Ways of Learning

Learning theories
and learning styles
in the classroom

Third edition

Alan Pritchard

Routledge
Taylor & Francis Group

LONDON AND NEW YORK

Third edition published 2014
by Routledge
2 Park Square, Milton Park, Abingdon, Oxon OX14 4RN

and by Routledge
711 Third Avenue, New York, NY 10017

Routledge is an imprint of the Taylor & Francis Group, an informa business

© 2014 A. Pritchard

First edition published 2005 by David Fulton Publishers
Second edition published 2009 by Routledge.

British Library Cataloguing in Publication Data
A catalogue record for this book is available from the British Library

Library of Congress Cataloging in Publication Data
Pritchard, Alan (Alan M.)
Ways of learning : learning theories and learning styles in the classroom /
Alan Pritchard. — Third edition.
    pages cm
ISBN 978–0–415–83492–6 (hardback) —
ISBN 978–0–415–83493–3 (paperback) —
ISBN 978–1–315–85208–9 (e-book)
1. Learning, Psychology of.   2. Cognitive styles.   I. Title.
LB1060.P735 2013
370.15′23—dc23

                                                    2013025066

ISBN: 978–0–415–83492–6 (hbk)
ISBN: 978–0–415–83493–3 (pbk)
ISBN: 978–1–315–85208–9 (ebk)

Typeset in Bembo
by RefineCatch Limited, Bungay, Suffolk

MIX
Paper from
responsible sources
FSC
www.fsc.org   FSC® C013056

Printed and bound in Great Britain by
TJ International Ltd, Padstow, Cornwall

To Mum and Dad, who set me on the road to learning, and to Jackie, Maria and Frances, who have taught me far more than I ever could have imagined possible. Even now, the learning continues.

Contents

Preface

Learning is something that happens quite naturally and goes by quite unnoticed in many cases. We may reflect on the way that a child is able to do something that previously they could not, and we may be amazed at the way that a young child has developed over even a short period of time. This is unplanned learning – though parents often spend time helping children to develop certain skills and understanding – and, as such, it is recognised as different from the planned learning that takes place in the more formal settings of our educational system: playgroups, nurseries and schools.

As children develop, they follow what is sometimes considered a 'normal' pattern of learning, and they become more skilled and knowledgeable almost as a matter of course. However, in order to enhance this process, we have an established system whereby children are taught and where they are initiated into the accepted knowledge and skills base that is considered to be essential if they are to grow into citizens of our society who are able to function and contribute effectively, as well as lead happy and fulfilling lives.

The nature of the accepted knowledge and skills is not a topic for consideration here, but the means by which the initiation takes place – in particular, the ways in which learning progresses and the most effective approaches that teachers might employ – are at the heart of this book. Learning in schools does not happen by chance, though children will learn many things that are not planned for, and an understanding of the ways in which we believe learning takes place is really essential for those responsible for planning and implementing programmes of learning: teachers.

Our understanding of the processes involved in learning is developing as more and more focused research is undertaken. This research takes place both in laboratories remote from schools and in classrooms, where teachers are engaging daily with an enormous range of topics and with an enormously variable population of learners. In the laboratories, the research might focus on the structure of the brain, for example, while, in classrooms, the research might focus on techniques of questioning or perhaps the effect of the immediate environment on the ability of children to concentrate. When all of the findings, however tentative some of them might be, are considered together, and when some of the assumptions from research are tested and re-examined in more detail, we are able to arrive at a generally accepted set of approaches to teaching that seem to be effective. This set of approaches is wide, variable and constantly shifting. That is to say, there is not a one-size-fits-all answer to the questions 'How do children learn?' and 'How should teachers teach?'

The purpose of this book is to review what is known about the ways that learning can take place and to present the views and theories of those researchers and practitioners who have been able to make detailed studies of the processes and complexities involved in learning – that is, gaining knowledge, developing understanding and acquiring skills.

We will consider some of the earliest attempts to understand learning, beginning with the behaviourist approaches made at the turn of the twentieth century. These theories have proved effective in providing approaches to teaching over many years, but, in a large number of areas, have been superseded by theories that take a broader stance on such things as mental activity, the importance of prior knowledge, social context and social interaction through the medium of language. An individual's preferred manner of working – learning style – is also an area of investigation that has developed to the point where it is possible to describe and observe what are sometimes quite big differences in the ways in which learners might make progress according to the ways in which they are expected to work. We will consider the more recent findings of research into the structure and functioning of the brain and look at the ways in which an understanding of the physiology, as opposed to the psychology, of the brain can lead to changes in the ways that we develop teaching strategies that we perceive as effective.

At each stage, we will look at some of the practical implications of the research and beliefs that are disseminated and promoted by those working in the different fields of educational development and other related disciplines. For teachers, the most important aspects of the findings of research are related to what they can do in their planning and teaching in order to improve and enhance the learning experiences and outcomes of those in their educational charge. When teaching is based soundly on the best available understanding of the processes that lead to effective learning, it has a greatly improved chance of being effective. Effective learning is learning that is lasting and capable of being put to use in new and differing situations. This book aims to provide that best available understanding. In doing so, the hope is that teachers might be able to provide even better learning opportunities for their pupils.

Preface to the third edition

In the years since the first edition of *Ways of Learning* was proposed and then published, the world of thinking in education – and the essential cognate areas of psychology, neuroscience, neuropsychology and, to a certain extent, philosophy – has moved on in a way that we should really expect it to, given both the centrality and importance of education to the world at large and the emphasis placed upon making 'improvements' to the systems in place. These improvements could be described as being put in place for political reasons by those who control and, sometimes, by those who practice education. Research has continued and the writing of both established academics and of newer researchers and practitioners has provided new insights into the ways and means of learning that lie at the heart of this book. New discoveries and recommendations in the field of neuroscience and neuropsychology have, in particular, shaped new views that are of importance to practitioners, and rightly so. Notions of learning style have come under scrutiny, and the ideas of early writers, such as Dewey, have been revisited and assessed in the light of twenty-first-century education.

Other revisions and additions in this third edition will reflect the comments and suggestions of readers who have contacted me. I am grateful for their comments; I hope they will serve to improve what I have written.

I am both surprised and happy to be able to revisit and, I hope, improve by fine tuning and additions a book that, I am told, has proved to be helpful in a wide range of teaching and learning settings. I am told that *Ways of Learning* has been found useful in pre-training, training and post-experience contexts, as an introduction for those studying learning and educational contexts at a higher level, but who come from a non-educational background, and by professions as diverse as paediatric doctors and nurses and web developers. I am astonished that a book that began life as a chapter in one of my previous books dealing with the use of the Internet as a learning tool is now in its third incarnation. I hope that it doesn't disappoint.

Alan Pritchard, Coventry, April 2013

Acknowledgements

I would like to thank all of those who took time to comment on the earlier editions of this book. Your comments have improved it. Specifically, I would like to include students, colleagues, Maggie Vance in Sheffield (who pointed out a serious gap in Chapter Six of the second edition, and then helped me to fill it) and a raft of reviewers, some known to me and some anonymous. Close family have played a part, too – Dad, Jackie, Maria and Frances have read it (at least 'parts' of it, in some cases) and told me what they think. I suspect that Chris may have sneaked a look, too; Rob may well have immersed himself in Chapter Six by now as well. Amazing!

1 Learning

Learning is something about which we all have an understanding and in which we have all participated. This participation will have been in a very wide range of settings, both formal and informal, and ranging from, for example, the relative confines of a school classroom to the wide open spaces of the countryside, or a quiet corner where a chance conversation led to deeper understanding of some topic or another.

Learning is not exclusive to the domain of an education system. Learning begins a very long time before school; continues for even longer after school; and happens rapidly, and in parallel with school, in a great number of different ways and settings. Learning proceeds in a number of different ways, and has been described and explained by many different interested researchers and opinion-makers over many years.

How is 'learning' currently defined?

Without looking for too long, and without delving too deeply into learned sources, it is possible to find a range of definitions of the process of learning. Table 1.1 contains a sample of these definitions.

TABLE 1.1 Definitions of learning

- A change in behaviour as a result of experience or practice.
- The acquisition of knowledge.
- Knowledge gained through study.
- To gain knowledge of, or skill in, something through study, teaching, instruction or experience.
- The process of gaining knowledge. A process by which behaviour is changed, shaped or controlled.
- The individual process of constructing understanding based on experience from a wide range of sources.

Each of us will identify more or less strongly with different definitions from the list presented. In everyday terms, it is supposed that learning is the process of gaining more knowledge, or of learning how to do something – ride a bike, for example. As we will see, learning is viewed differently by those who have spent time investigating and experimenting in the field, according to the context of their work and other factors exerting influence at the time. We will look at the work of both behaviourists and cognitive psychologists and consider the very different approaches that each takes and the very different definitions that each might offer of a process that, for most of us, comes very naturally.

A basic understanding of processes of learning is essential for those who intend to develop activities that will have the potential to lead to effective learning taking place in classrooms; that is, teachers. In more recent times, there has been a reduction in the emphasis given to learning about 'learning', from a theoretical standpoint, in initial courses for teacher education in the UK. This has been for a variety of reasons. For example, in recent years, there has been a proliferation of regulations from central government that have made great demands on the training providers and substantially squeezed the time available for teaching. There has also been an emergence of alternative entry routes into teaching, some of which can be called 'work based'. This, too, has led to a reduction of the time available for theoretical work. To be fair, and in the view of most of those involved in teacher education, the balance between practice and theory has been improved, but this has been at the expense of some areas of teaching that have traditionally made up the curriculum for initial training courses.

The last years of the twentieth century and the first decade or so of the twenty-first have seen a great deal of regulation aimed at the institutions responsible for the training of teachers. There has also been a shift towards more school-based training through various schemes, which has, to some extent, had the effect of reducing the amount of what could be called 'taught input'. The latest incarnation of school-based training is the School Direct scheme, which offers school-based 'on the job' training for 'high-quality' graduates (DfE 2012a), either with a sizeable bursary or with a salary. In tandem with this, there has been a big increase in the level of accountability to the Government, through the medium of the Teacher Training Agency (later renamed the Training and Development Agency for Schools; later still, reconfigured as the Teaching Agency; and now operating as the National College for Teaching and Leadership) and through the inspection of teacher training by the Office for Standards in Education (Ofsted). This has been a political drive towards raising standards in schools; improving the quality of teachers; and arriving at consistency and uniformity among the trainers, which had previously been missing. Another, more recent initiative, which has expanded greatly since the election of the Conservative government in 2010, is the introduction of academy status schools, whereby schools can fully opt out of local authority control.

One of the many outcomes of these reforms seems to have been that teachers in training are not always fully introduced to more than introductory ideas of learning theory, which underpin the approaches taken by effective teachers. In some cases, trainees are not always introduced to recent and current ideas relating to learning, such as those that are considered in later chapters of this book. Though only anecdotal, it seems that some recently qualified teachers, when introduced to basic ideas from learning theory as a part of a higher degree programme of continuing professional development, have expressed surprise that this had not been covered in their initial training. Some would argue that initial training is not the place to dwell on what can be seen as uncontextualised theory, and that after some time in post, when theory can be related very directly to practice, is the best time to consider theory or, at least, to revisit it.

The current standards that trainee teachers have to meet in order to obtain qualified teacher status (QTS) do not explicitly refer to learning theory, but some of the standards, if they are to be met effectively, rely on more than a passing familiarity with theory and research (DfE 2012b). For example, in Part One: Teaching of the standards document, it is stated that teachers must 'demonstrate knowledge and understanding of how pupils learn and how this impacts on teaching' (DfE 2012b). Related to this, the standards document also sets out that teachers should be able to 'promote a love of learning and children's intellectual curiosity' as well as having a 'secure understanding of how a range of factors can inhibit pupils' ability to learn' (DfE 2012b). It seems fairly obvious that teachers need to know about and understand the mechanics of the learning process, and this is reinforced, by statute, in the regulations contained in the Teachers' Standards document.

We need to be aware that strategies are not the same as theory. Theory is something that is able to explain what is observed, upon which strategies – what is actually done in the classroom to achieve particular learning outcomes – are based. Certainly, it is possible to teach would-be teachers a range of approaches (strategies) to adopt in their work with children, and this will lead to trainees having knowledge of the strategies under consideration, but to approach this teaching without considering the underlying theory would be to leave the job only half completed and provide the trainees with little understanding of the reasons for such approaches.

A brief historical perspective

Although the history of a philosophical interest in learning can be traced back to ancient Greece, the modern history of the psychology of learning dates back to the late nineteenth and early twentieth centuries. William James, an American philosopher and physician, is considered to have been in at the very beginning of the serious study of mental processes. He said, in 1890, that psychology was the 'science of mental life'. It is from this approximate starting point that the study of the mind and of human behaviour – and, in particular, the study of learning – began to grow.

Early interest in learning, or training, was centred purely on behaviour. As we will see, the followers of this work developed the area of learning psychology referred to as 'behaviourism'. Behaviourism developed rapidly through the early years of the twentieth century, and almost, but not quite, alongside this growing interest in behaviour and the modification of behaviour came the growing realisation that the unseen mental processes involved in learning, and the contribution of factors apart from environmental rewards or gratification, had an important bearing on the understanding of how we learn.

So, in very general terms, two branches of the psychology of learning developed and have made important inroads into the practice of teaching over recent decades. First, there is behaviourism; second, 'constructivism', which is an aspect of a very much larger field of understanding and study, that of cognitive psychology. Both of these branches have a series of sub-branches, but it is reasonably fair to divide learning theory in this way. As we will see, behaviourism is concerned with what can be seen happening – behaviour. Constructivism rests on the idea that knowledge and, more importantly, understanding are constructed by individual learners and an understanding of the mental processes involved; the underlying structures relating to knowledge and understanding are deemed to be of prime importance.

Other developments

An aspect of the learning process that, in relative terms, has only recently come to the fore is that of individual learning preferences. The ideas that lie behind the notion that we, as individual learners, have preferred approaches to our learning, are based upon research that identifies humans as more or less receptive to different stimuli. For example, one learner might find it particularly straightforward to take in information through one particular medium while another learner would find this quite difficult. This leads to a classification of learning types, which describes learners in such terms as 'visual' or 'auditory' learners, to name but two. Other researchers have developed other types of classifications that emphasise other characteristics. This whole area of individual preference, or propensity for different approaches to learning, has the potential to make a big impact on what happens in classrooms. Work continues to establish the efficacy of looking at learners in this way, with some researchers considering that it is perhaps less helpful than others. Naturally, as time moves on, and evidence accumulates, the value of certain accepted views is questioned, and this is the case with learning style research and thinking, as we will see.

An important development in our understanding of how learning proceeds was the publication of Howard Gardner's work on what he has called 'multiple intelligences' (1983). He describes a picture of a set of different intelligence strengths – including areas such as linguistic, mathematical, physical and more – that we all have in different proportions, giving each of us a different profile of intelligences that will affect the way in which we approach problems and the ease with which we might understand new ideas according to how they are presented.

Metacognition is another example of the development of our realisation that learning is a vast and complex subject. 'Metacognition' refers to knowledge and thought about thinking and learning itself. It is proposed that if an individual learner is able to gain insight into their own thought processes and come to understand better the ways in which they learn, then they are better equipped as learners and likely to make good progress at times when they might otherwise find learning less than straightforward.

The last developing area of knowledge about learning that we will highlight here (and consider in more detail in Chapter 7) is that of what has been termed 'brain-based learning', which is not a good term for the burgeoning area of research that is now, even more than at the time of publication of the first and second editions of this book, forging important links between psychology, neuroscience and the everyday practicalities of learning. Accordingly, the term 'brain-based learning' has fallen, recently, into disuse and the area of study linking neuroscience and education has a new name: neuroeducational research.

Neuropsychology is defined as the study of the relationship between brain functioning and abilities such as memory, attention, language and reasoning (Fuchs, 2009), and, as such, it is a branch of psychology that studies the links between the structure and function of the brain and behaviour. It is, then, the area of study that deals with the relationship between our body's nervous system – in particular, the brain – and higher order mental functions, such as those relating to language, memory, and perception, and the ways in which what we do – specifically, learning, in the context of this book – is controlled and affected by both the structure of the brain and the way that it functions. This is a massive, intriguing and rapidly developing domain.

Clearly, neuropsychology has a very close, even intimate relationship to how we consider learning. Neuropsychology draws heavily on neuroscience research, and, in recent years, this has led to many advances and to new light being shed upon old precepts. There has been a move towards putting to rest what have become known as the 'myths of brain-based learning' whilst, at the same time, informing new ideas about learning and the structure and behaviour of the brain.

2

Behaviourism and the beginnings of theory

The ideas of behaviourism have their roots in the late nineteenth and early twentieth centuries, although it is possible to trace some ideas back to Thomas Hobbes (1588–1679) and David Hume (1711–76). John Watson (1878–1958), an American working in the realm of this new philosophy of psychology, is widely accepted as one of the earliest proponents of behaviourism. He is believed to have first used the term 'behaviourism' (though he probably used the American spelling). Watson came to the view that psychology could only ever become a true science if it became a process of detailed objective observation and scientific measurement. This notion of observation and measurement became central to the work of behaviourists. Any consideration of mental process, which is by definition unobservable, fell outside their self-imposed range of interest. So, behaviourist approaches to, and explanations of, learning developed out of the study of what can actually be seen. As we will see, this approach to developing a psychological theory of learning ignores much of the hidden mental process that later workers in the field have come to explain and to hold as crucially important to our understanding of the complex activity that makes up different types of learning. Advances in neuroimaging techniques, as we will see later, make this an even more important element of any work investigating learning.

Behaviourism is based around the central notion of a reaction being made to a particular stimulus. This apparently simple relationship has been used to describe even the most complex learning situations. At its simplest, we can observe behaviour, which we can refer to as 'learnt behaviour', in a wide range of diverse situations. For example, a performing seal will respond to a particular stimulus – the sound of a hooter or the presentation of a fish – by raising itself up and slapping its flippers together as if clapping. A pet dog will respond to the stimulus of the spoken word, 'Beg', by doing just that, much to the delight of onlookers.

This stimulus–response relationship can also be seen in humans. In situations where an immediate response is required, practice situations are repeated endlessly so that the soldier, firefighter or airline pilot will make the correct, possibly lifesaving, response in a given situation. The importance of responsive practice has been underlined in more recent years, and explained in terms of the reinforcement of particular neural pathways in the brain, which has the effect of faster and smoother implementation of certain actions and responses. The adage 'practice makes perfect' seems to hold good for behaviourists, and also may have resonances for neuropsychologists. In schools, we notice an obvious response to the signal marking the end of a lesson. No matter how many times the teacher might remind a class that the bell is a signal for the teacher, the class can hardly restrain themselves from collecting their pens and pencils together ready to leave. Also in the classroom, a child might respond to the stimulus of the question, 'What are seven eights?' with the automatic response, '56'. This immediate 'correct' response will be made if the connection between the stimulus and response has been built correctly in the first instance, and subsequently reinforced over time; the associated neural pathways have been practised and strengthened. It should be noted here that making a 'correct' response does not necessarily imply understanding. In the same way as a parrot might react to the question, 'How are you?' with the response, 'I'm fine', so a child correctly responding with '56' need not necessarily understand the significance of the reply. Behaviourism is based upon the simple notion of a relationship between a stimulus and a response, which is why behaviourist theories are often referred to as 'stimulus–response' theories.

Behaviourism: a definition

'Behaviourism is a theory of animal and human learning that focuses upon the behaviour of the learner and the change in behaviour that occurs when learning takes place.' (Woollard 2010) It is a theory of learning focusing on observable behaviours and discounting any mental activity. Learning is defined simply as the acquisition of new behaviour.

Behaviourists call this method of learning 'conditioning'. Two different types of conditioning are described and demonstrated as viable explanations of the way in which animals and humans alike can be 'taught' to do certain things. First, there is classical conditioning.

Classical conditioning

This involves the reinforcement of a natural reflex or some other behaviour that occurs as a response to a particular stimulus. A well-known example of this type of conditioning, the first of its kind, is the work of Ivan Pavlov, a Russian physiologist who, at the start of the twentieth century, conditioned dogs to salivate at the sound of a bell. He noticed that dogs salivated when they ate, or even saw, food. In his initial experiments, he sounded a bell at the time when food was presented to the dogs. The sound of the bell became, for the dogs, an indication that food was about to be presented, and, eventually, the dogs would salivate at the sound of the bell, irrespective of the presence of food. The dogs had been conditioned to respond to the sound of the bell by producing saliva. Their behaviour had been successfully modified.

We talk about conditioning and conditioned responses in a general way. Feelings of fear at the sound of a dentist's drill or at the sight of a syringe in preparation for an injection are examples of conditioned responses.

Pavlov identified four stages in the process of his classical conditioning and what follows from the initial connection between stimulus and response: acquisition, extinction, generalisation and discrimination.

Acquisition

The 'acquisition' phase is the initial learning of the conditioned response – for example, the dog salivating at the sound of the bell.

Extinction

Once learnt, a conditioned response will not remain indefinitely. 'Extinction' is used to describe the disappearance of the conditioned response brought about by repeatedly presenting the bell, for example, without then presenting food.

Generalisation

After a conditioned response to one stimulus has been learnt, it may also respond to similar stimuli without further training. If a child is bitten by a dog, the child may fear not only that particular dog, but all dogs.

Discrimination

'Discrimination' is the opposite of generalisation. An individual learns to produce a conditioned response to one stimulus, but not to another, similar stimulus. For example, a child may show a fear response to freely roaming dogs, but show no fear when a dog is on a lead, or distrust Alsatians but not Jack Russell terriers.

Operant conditioning

The second type of conditioning is 'operant conditioning'. Operant conditioning is the most important type of behaviourist learning. It is more flexible in its nature than classical conditioning, and, therefore, seen as potentially more powerful. It involves reinforcing a behaviour by rewarding it. It can also work in a negative way, when an undesirable behaviour can be discouraged, by following it with punishment of some form. In some cases, simply not offering an expected reward for a particular behaviour is a sufficient punishment. For example, if a mother gives her child a chocolate bar every day that he tidies his bedroom, before long, the child may spend some time each day tidying. In this example, the tidying behaviour increases because it is rewarded. This rewarding is known as 'reinforcement'. It is likely that the tidying behaviour would decrease or stop completely if the rewards were suspended.

B. F. Skinner (1904–90), a psychologist working in America in the 1930s, is the most famous psychologist in the field of operant conditioning and probably the most famous behaviourist. Skinner studied the behaviour of rats and pigeons, and made generalisations of his discoveries to humans. He used a device now called a Skinner box; a simple, empty box in which an animal could earn food by making simple responses, such as pressing a lever. A normal, almost random action by the animal, such as pressing a lever in the box, would result in a reward, such as a pellet of food. As the rewards continued for the repetition of the action, the animal 'learnt' that, in order to be fed, it must press the lever.

Skinner maintained that rewards and punishments control the majority of human behaviours, and that the principles of operant conditioning can explain all human learning (1958). The key aspects of operant conditioning are as follows.

Reinforcement

This refers to anything that has the effect of strengthening a particular behaviour and makes it likely that the behaviour will happen again. There are two types of reinforcement: positive and negative.

Positive reinforcement
Positive reinforcement is a powerful method for controlling the behaviour of both animals and people. For people, positive reinforcers include basic items, such as food, drink, approval or even something as apparently simple as attention. In the context of classrooms, praise, house points or the freedom to choose an activity are all used in different contexts as rewards for desirable behaviour.

Negative reinforcement
As its name suggests, this is a method of decreasing the likelihood of a behaviour by pairing it with an unpleasant 'follow up'. There is controversy about whether punishment is an effective way of reducing or eliminating unwanted behaviours. Laboratory experiments have shown that punishment can be an effective method for reducing particular behaviour, but there are clear disadvantages, too, especially in classroom situations. Anger, frustration or aggression may follow punishment, or there may be other negative emotional responses.

Shaping

The notion of shaping refers to a technique of reinforcement that is used to teach animals or humans behaviours that they have never performed before. When shaping, the trainer begins by reinforcing a simple response that the learner can easily perform. Gradually, more and more complex responses are required for the same reward. For example, to teach a rat to press an overhead lever, the trainer can first reward any upward head movement, then an upward movement of at least three centimetres, then six and so on until the lever is reached. Shaping has been used to teach children with severe mental difficulties to speak by first rewarding any sounds they make, and then gradually only rewarding sounds that approximate to the words being taught. Animal trainers use shaping to teach their charges. In classrooms, shaping can be used to teach progressively complex skills, and more obviously to ensure the desired behaviour from children at such times as the end of the day, lining up for assembly and so on. When a teacher says something like, 'Let's see which table is ready', it would not be unusual in many classrooms to witness many, if not all, of the children sitting up straight with folded arms, having tidied away their belongings.

There is a place for learning in classrooms that relies on the principles of behaviourism. However, since behaviourism gives little importance to mental activity, concept formation or understanding, there are difficult problems to overcome when setting out philosophies of teaching and learning that depend wholly upon behaviourist approaches.

Behaviourism in general learning situations

As all parents will understand, there are certain situations where, for reasons of safety, it is important that young children do not do certain things – stepping off the kerb, poking electrical sockets, reaching towards a pan of cooking vegetables and so on. In a potentially dangerous situation, a parent is likely to respond swiftly and decisively. Often, the action taken by a parent will involve a shouted 'No!' or the rapid removal of the child from the situation. The child will come to associate the poking of an electrical socket with an undesirable reaction from the parent, and, in this way, learn to avoid the reaction by not poking sockets – at least, that is the expectation. The reason for no longer carrying out socket poking is not dependent upon an understanding of the dangers of electrocution. The cessation of the poking behaviour can be described in terms of negative reinforcement. Had the parental response to the action been a smile and a hug, it is possible that the action would be positively reinforced and the chances of repetition increased significantly. This is not to recommend shouting, smacking or any such extreme action, but it can be seen that for reasons of expediency and future safety, a behaviourist response serves well. Indeed, attempting to explain the nature of possible outcomes from particular actions becomes very difficult when such concepts as severe injury or death come into the equation. The eradication of the behaviour is the most important consideration; the concepts involved become far less important. Some might argue that knowing to do or not to do something is, initially at least, far more important than understanding; the understanding can follow along behind at a more appropriate time in the intellectual development of the child.

Behaviourism in 'school learning'

To apply models of behaviourism in the classroom, it is necessary to have clear ideas of the behaviours (operants) to be encouraged and reinforced. These behaviours could be either related to general behaviour (in the 'good/bad behaviour' sense of the word), or more educational content related (spellings, tables and so on). The nature of the reinforcement also needs to be established. Rewards can be widely variable in nature: ticks and written comments in books; stars, stamps and stickers; more formal points or commendations, possibly leading to higher level rewards such as certificates; verbal and public praise; extra privileges; sweets.

Considerations for the use of rewards

- The rewards need to have value to the children.
- If rewards come unexpectedly, intrinsic motivation will remain high.
- If extrinsic rewards are used, it is important that everyone receives one for their best efforts. Rewarding only the 'best' is not a satisfactory approach, as it is vital to maintain high self-esteem, especially with the less able and lower attaining children.
- Rewards can be used to invigorate or add fun to an activity.

Problems in using extrinsic rewards

- Rewards can belittle or demean a learning experience.
- Rewards can engender feelings of unfairness or competition.
- Rewards can detract from the real issue involved in completing tasks.
- Rewards do not always lead to higher quality work.
- Rewards may isolate children who feel they have little chance of getting a reward.

Critics of the application of behaviourist approaches make two main points. First, that rewarding children for all learning is likely to cause the child to lose interest in learning for its own sake. Studies have suggested that using rewards with children who are already well motivated may lead to a loss of interest in the subject. Second, using a reward system or giving one child increased attention may have a detrimental effect on the others in the class. Using a behaviourist approach in the classroom seems to be most effective when applied in cases where a particular child has a history of academic failure; where there is very low motivation and high anxiety; and in cases where no other approach has worked.

Teachers find – and research (for example, Elliott and Busse 1991) also indicates – that rewarding aids the reinforcement of appropriate classroom behaviours, such as paying attention and treating others well; decreases misbehaviour; and makes for a more orderly atmosphere that is conducive to learning. The creation and maintaining of a supportive atmosphere conducive to work and attainment is a prerequisite for effective teaching. Previously, the standards that applied to the award of QTS in the UK required that trainee teachers demonstrate that they are able to: 'demonstrate [the] positive values' (Standard Q2) and 'establish a purposeful and safe learning environment conducive to learning' (Standard Q30) (TDA 2007). Subtle behaviourist approaches can be a useful tool for teachers in this area of their role. Since the rationalisation of the standards required of teachers that came into effect in 2012 (DfE 2012b), the wording of the requirements has been altered and slimmed down somewhat, but it is still clear that the points made in the preceding standards document remain valid, even if they are not made explicit in the current incarnation of the regulations for teacher training.

Since it seems to be the case that, the more often a stimulus and response occur in association with each other, the stronger the habit will become, a concentration on repetition seems to be a reasonable approach to take in certain learning situations. This repetition is seen in the drill and practice tutorials often associated with the learning of basic skills. An example of behaviourism taking on a major role in a drill and practice situation came with the onset of the introduction of computers into classrooms. With 'drill and practice' software, children are routinely presented with several answers to a question, and, with each correct response, they receive some type of positive reinforcement (a smiley face, more 'fuel', or more 'bullets' to fire). With each incorrect response, children are, at best, given the opportunity to review the material before attempting to answer the question once again, or, at worst, given the equivalent of a punishment in the form of a non-smiley face, the loss of points or some such undesirable outcome. These types of programs allow children of varying abilities to work on exercises in their own time and at their own pace. In this way, it is said, all can achieve a similar level of competence and teacher time can be spent on teaching more complex knowledge and skills, or focusing on those children with particular needs. It has to be said that many children do find this style of presentation of work motivating, and, for some, the learning benefits, in terms of test scores, for example, are clear. There are, as we have seen, questions concerning understanding and conceptual development. The use of individualised, behaviouristic learning, mediated by computers and in the form of an integrated learning system (ILS) has become a feature of some developments in ICT-supported learning environments, as we will see later.

Skinner urged educators to focus on reinforcement and on success, rather than on punishing failure. In many cases, those who benefit most from approaches based on behaviourist notions are those who are less well motivated, have high anxiety or a history of failure. It must be remembered that these techniques do not work well for everyone. Bright children can find programmed instruction or simplistic drill and practice situations unsatisfying and even boring. Some children crave understanding and find answers without understanding difficult and frustrating.

The idea of learning without understanding, mentioned briefly above, has at times been transported directly into the classroom. Some readers may well remember being told how to divide one vulgar fraction by another by turning one of the fractions 'upside down' and then multiplying them together. This approach to teaching and being able to achieve right answers is fine for some, but for others it seems like some sort of voodoo spell and can lead to a high level of frustration. Some need to know why certain apparent 'tricks' work; without understanding the logic, they cannot operate. This was summed up by the maths educator Arnold Howell when he quoted, ironically, a not uncommon rhyme used to help remember the trick for dividing one fraction by another: 'Ours is not to reason why, just invert and multiply.'

Behaviourism, then, is based on the idea that learning is a change in behaviour, and that changes in behaviour occur as a response to a stimulus of one kind or another. The response leads to a consequence, and, when the consequence is pleasant and positive, then the behaviour change is reinforced. With consistent reinforcement, the behaviour pattern becomes conditioned.

An example might involve teaching a child to say 'please' and 'thank you' appropriately. If the child is hungry and sitting at the table, the parent might have the child say, 'please' when offered food and 'thank you' when it is taken. If 'please' is not said, the food is withheld. When 'please' is finally articulated by the child, the food is served. Over the course of many meals, the child's response to the stimulus becomes conditioned and a lifelong pattern of saying 'please' and 'thank you' at suitable times becomes established.

Many modern learning theorists and educationalists discount a great deal of behaviourist theory. However, there are situations where a behaviourist approach is likely to work well. Programmed learning was developed out of the theories of Skinner and others, and became a fashionable and partly successful approach to teaching in the middle part of the last century. Skinner (1958) described the purpose of programmed learning as being to 'manage human learning under controlled conditions'. In practice, this would mean that a textbook or, as the technology allowed, a computer presents material to be learnt in a series of small steps, with each step known as a 'frame'. Each frame would contain an item of information and a statement with a blank space to be completed by the learner. The correct answer would next be uncovered by moving a paper down the page, or by some such process, before the learner would move on to the next frame. Each frame would introduce a new idea or review what had gone before. The learner's response, compared with the uncovered answer, serves to reinforce correct responses, making it likely that they will be repeated and internalised. The process of shaping is employed, in that the programme of learning starts from the learner's initial knowledge, then moves forwards in small increments. The learner is usually, as a result of the progression being made in very small steps, able to give accurate and correct responses that are continually positively reinforced, which will have the effect of keeping motivation high. Skinner emphasised the reinforcement given by the 'machine' for every correct response, and the importance of immediate feedback.

Behaviourism is clearly at the heart of, and the key to the success of, programmed learning. In more recent times, ILSs have made use of the behaviourist tradition and of the processing power of modern computers to provide individualised routes through learning materials. Today, an ILS is a computer-based system used for teaching. Lessons are organised by level of difficulty and worked through progressively by an individual learner. An ILS also includes a number of management tools for assessment, record keeping, report writing and for providing other user information files that help to identify learning needs, monitor progress and maintain records.

By repeatedly presenting information in small amounts and by reinforcing correct responses, the ILS is operating in a way that can be traced back directly to Skinner's ideas. Becker (1993) identifies the behaviourist '*programmed learning* theories of Skinner and others as those which underpin the model of learning used by Integrated Learning Systems. These theories assume the child's learning is solitary and individualistic.' Purcell (n.d.) points out that 'behaviourist ideas of learning certainly match the style of teaching and learning associated with the use of Integrated Learning Systems'.

The behaviourist approach that seems to be at the heart of ILSs has been a cause of concern for many; the apparent lack of understanding that is engendered by the process is also cause for concern. However, certain elements of the results in standardised tests in both literacy and numeracy have shown marked increases, in many cases, where ILSs have been evaluated (Underwood and Brown 1997; Underwood *et al.* 1994).

In the early days of computer use in schools, there were many examples of educational software designed wholly around behaviourist principles, as we saw earlier. Challenges would be set in spelling or in arithmetic, and a correct answer would activate a jingle and a flashing picture to indicate success. An incorrect answer would result, at best, in nothing, but, at worst, in a condemnation in the form of a screen picture of maybe a dunce's cap accompanied by an appropriate sound effect. The simplicity of many of the programs led to an approach of trial and error, or even random selection, by a number of users, and the use of this type of program was condemned by some. For example, Daniel Chandler (1984) considered that 'The microcomputer is a tool of awesome potency which is making it possible for educational practice to take a giant step backwards'. Others have seen the benefits to particular individuals and groups of children. This is perhaps an indication that the adoption of a blanket, one-size-fits-all approach is not appropriate when we are considering the learning experiences we provide for children.

Behaviourism in practice

In addition to using behaviourist methods in certain teaching situations, the methods can also be effective in establishing classroom behaviours. In a classroom environment, the teacher identifies the behaviours that are desirable and the behaviours that would be best discouraged. It is a somewhat natural impulse to develop punishments for those behaviours that need to be discouraged, yet research has indicated that positive reinforcements have a stronger and longer-lasting effect. Therefore, instead of devising a punishment for undesired behaviour, a reward of some kind for the preferred behaviour should be devised. When the correct actions are taken – sitting quietly, not shouting out, forming an orderly line by the door – the child is rewarded. When the incorrect action shows up, the reward is withheld. The most important element in establishing rewards is that they must be relevant to the child and be equally available to everyone in the classroom. Another consideration is that the reward can be incredibly simple. For many young children, the approval of the teacher or some public display of simple praise is reward enough. In some classrooms, more regulated systems of reward work well. We have already considered the use of a system of points leading to stars on a chart, with the possibility of an end-of-term treat or the awarding of a smiley-faced sticker serving well. Teachers often devise their own schemes for reward, and some include the option to remove the reward, such as by deducting a point or removing the privilege in some way. The importance of a positive stance towards behaviour management is the crucial element of behaviourist 'control', and this seems to be emphasised by effective teachers. The influential Hay/McBer report (2000) tells us that an effective teacher 'uses rewards to influence behaviour and performance positively.'

Self-paced learning modules can be designed to take advantage of behaviourist principles. A learning experience that gives frequent feedback while the child 'learns' the material in small, bite-sized pieces is much more likely to be successful than a learning experience that simply consists of extensive reading with an end-of-term test as the only form of assessment. To further increase the likelihood of success, content can be arranged in such a manner as to 'steer' the child towards correct responses. Early success is likely to increase a child's self-esteem and add to the child's motivation to carry on. While some may find this method to be overly helpful, or think of it as too much handholding, the end result is that the child has accomplished the goal and been able to meet specific learning objectives as planned. It is certainly the case that if behaviourist approaches were to be totally disregarded in planning for learning, a certain measure of what has been shown to be effective would be lost. However, as we will consider in later chapters, there are other theoretical perspectives that, in all probability, have more importance to the majority of learning situations, which teachers will be keen to establish. Behaviourism has a place in planning that teachers undertake, but it should most certainly not be relied upon alone as a perspective from which to plan all teaching and learning.

Having spent some time in what could be considered as an educational wilderness, behaviourism has had a certain revival in recent years, albeit a mini revival. It may be a function of the harsh expectations placed on teachers for better and better 'results', or it may be caused by some other changes in thinking and a new look at research from the past as well as more recent studies. For an overview of more current thinking, and of the historical perspectives presented below, see Woollard (2010).

A history of the names associated with behaviourism

Pavlov

Pavlov developed the theory known now as 'classical conditioning' through the study of dogs. From his perspective, learning begins with a stimulus–response connection. In this theory, a certain stimulus leads to a particular response.

Thorndike

Edward Thorndike (1874–1949) introduced a theory of learning now called 'connectionism'. He emphasised the role of experience in the strengthening and weakening of stimulus–response connections: 'Responses to a situation that are followed by satisfaction are strengthened; responses that are followed by discomfort, weakened.' Thorndike proposed that practice also influences stimulus–response connections. His idea that rewards promote learning continues to be a key element of behaviourist theory.

Watson

Watson introduced the term 'behaviourism' and was an important advocate of the approach in the early part of the twentieth century. He called for the use of scientific objectivity and experiment in the psychology of learning. He also devised the law of frequency, which stresses the importance of repetition: 'The more frequent a stimulus and response occur in association with each other, the stronger that habit will become.' He devised the law of recency, too: 'The response that has most recently occurred after a particular stimulus is the response most likely to be associated with that stimulus.'

Guthrie

Edwin Guthrie (1886–1959) put forward a theory of what he called 'contiguity': 'A stimulus that is followed by a particular response will, upon its recurrence, tend to be followed by the same response again. This stimulus–response connection gains in its full strength on one trial.' Guthrie conducted very little practical research, and, as a result, doubt has been cast upon his theories.

Skinner

Skinner is probably the best-known psychologist in the behaviourist tradition. He identified the theory of operant conditioning. He spoke only about the strengthening of responses, not the strengthening of habits or actions. He used the term 'reinforcer' instead of 'reward'. He was keen to stress the importance of a positive approach to learning involving rewards, but also understood the value of punishment. His defining principle is his law of conditioning: 'A response followed by a reinforcing stimulus is strengthened and therefore more likely to occur again.' A second principle of note is his law of extinction: 'A response that is not followed by a reinforcing stimulus is weakened and therefore less likely to occur again.' Skinner's work was meticulous and methodical, based upon scrupulous scientific observation and measurement. He developed strict schedules of reinforcement in his attempt to codify learning and to establish a pattern of best practice. In his later work, he began to recognise the influence of mental process, which had previously been acknowledged by behaviourists.

Summary

Behaviourists see learning as a relatively permanent, observable change in behaviour as a result of experience. This change is effected through a process of reward and reinforcement, but has little regard, initially, for mental process or understanding.

In the classroom

- Standard routines and expectations for behaviour can be made clear and reinforced in a behaviouristic way.
- The use of rewards in the form of team points, or such like, can be a great incentive to work hard and to behave well.
- Punishments, such as loss of privileges or the withholding of rewards, can be effective as well, although it is widely recognised that a positive approach is preferable to an approach to behaviour management predicated solely on punishments.
- Some 'rote' learning may be a useful way of helping a number of children to cope better with various aspects of their work that they find difficult. Where possible, though, initial rote learning should be followed by attempts to encourage understanding.

It is interesting, in consideration of the basic tenets of behaviourist learning theory, to look briefly at a quotation from Lao-Tzu, an ancient Chinese philosopher of the sixth century: 'Rewards and punishments are the lowest form of education.' This leads conveniently into the next chapter, which deals with cognitive learning theory, where the place of reward and punishment is far less prominent.

3

Cognitive, constructivist learning

Constructivist theories

The area of constructivism, in the field of learning, comes under the broad heading of cognitive science. Cognitive science is an expansive area. It has its roots in the first half of the twentieth century, at a time when academics from the disciplines of psychology, artificial intelligence, philosophy, linguistics, neuroscience and anthropology realised that they were all trying to solve problems concerning the mind and the brain.

Cognitive science: a definition

Among other things, cognitive scientists study how people learn, remember and interact, often with a strong emphasis on mental processes and often with an emphasis on modern technologies. Cognitive science investigates 'intelligence and intelligent systems, with particular reference to intelligent behaviour' (Posner 1984).

Cognitive psychology: a definition

Cognitive psychology is the scientific study of mental processes such as learning, perceiving, remembering, using language, reasoning and solving problems.

Constructivism: a definition

Constructivists view learning as the result of mental construction. That is, learning takes place when new information is built into and added onto an individual's current structure of knowledge, understanding and skills. We learn best when we actively construct our own understanding.

The reference in the preceding paragraph to 'knowledge, understanding and skills' refers to what is commonly considered to be a description of the types of learning that we become involved with. These three areas for learning are joined by a fourth to become:

1 knowledge

2 concepts

3 skills

4 attitudes (DES 1985).

It is within these four areas that all learning – in particular, school learning – can be placed. We learn factual information; we learn to understand new ideas; we learn skills, both mental and physical; and we learn about, and develop, new attitudes to our environment.

Piaget

Jean Piaget (1896–1980), who is considered to be one of the most influential early proponents of a constructivist approach to understanding learning, is one of the best-known psychologists in the field of child development and learning. Many teachers are introduced to what is known as his 'developmental stage' theory, which sets out age-related developmental stages. The stages begin with the sensorimotor stage and end with the stage of formal operations. The developmental stage theory is a useful guide to intellectual growth, but more recent thinking has gone beyond Piaget's view. Table 3.1 sets out Piaget's stages.

Stages of development

During the sensorimotor stage, Piaget said that a child's cognitive system is more or less limited to motor reflexes that are present at birth, such as sucking. The child builds on these reflexes to develop more sophisticated behaviour. Children learn to generalise specific actions and activities to a wider range of situations and make use of them in increasingly complex patterns of behaviour.

At Piaget's preoperational stage, children acquire the ability to represent ideas and to engage in mental imagery. In particular, they do this through the medium of language. They have an egocentric view; that is, they view the world almost exclusively from their own point of view and find it difficult to consider situations from another's perspective, known as 'decentring'. A child choosing a cake because they know that they like the flavour, rather than because it is larger, is also an example of decentring.

In the concrete operational stage, children become more able to take another's point of view, and they begin to be able to take into account multiple perspectives. Although they can understand concrete problems, Piaget would argue that they cannot deal effectively with more abstract problems.

TABLE 3.1 Piaget's stages of development

Period	Age	Characteristics of the stage
Sensorimotor	0–2 years	Simple reflexive behaviour gives way to ability to form schemas and to create patterns and chains of behaviour. Over time, children come to realise that objects exist even if they cannot be seen.
Preoperational	2–7 years	Children are essentially egocentric and unable to consider events from another's point of view. The use of symbolic thought begins, and the imagination also begins to develop.
Concrete operational	7–11 years	Children begin to use logical thought about physical operations; they are able to 'conserve' – that is, they realise that two equal physical quantities remain equal even if the appearance of one changes.
Formal operations	11+ years	Children are able to think hypothetically and abstractly, although this is limited by lack of depth and breadth in knowledge.

At the stage of formal operations, children are capable of thinking logically and in the abstract. Piaget considered this stage to be the ultimate stage of intellectual development, and said that, although children were still in a position of having relatively little knowledge, their thought processes were as well developed as they were ever likely to be.

Whether Piaget was correct or not, it is safe to say that his theory of cognitive development has had a great influence on all work in the field of developmental psychology. His view of a child's intellectual development has influenced teaching practices, too. It gives teachers approximate guidance concerning the level of complexity that might be expected in a child's thought processes at approximate stages in their development. The exactness of the stage of development in relation to a child's age has been criticised; that is to say, a child may well pass through the stages, but it is not clear that they will pass through them at specific ages. However, as a developmental trail, it is useful.

Another aspect of Piaget's work is concerned with the growth of knowledge and understanding, and the ways in which new information is dealt with by young learners. Piaget's descriptions of assimilation and accommodation, which we will consider next, are not restricted to young learners, and give a good representation of the process of learning for learners of all ages.

Assimilation and accommodation

For Piaget, learning is a process of adjustment to environmental influences. He describes two basic processes that form this process of adjustment. They are 'assimilation' and 'accommodation'. Piaget's view is influenced by his background in biology, and he sees organisms, including human beings, as constantly seeking to maintain a stability in their existence. A physical example of this would be the maintenance of a constant body temperature. If external conditions change – get hotter, for example – a sophisticated organism will make physical changes in order to maintain stability. The body's temperature regulation systems come into operation and a constant temperature is held. Piaget's model for learning has resonances with this notion. External experiences can have an impact on what is already 'known'. It could be that a new experience can add to and reinforce 'knowledge' that is held, or it could contradict existing knowledge. For example, a young child might know that a small creature covered in fur, with four legs and having a tail is a dog. The more examples of dogs that the child comes across, the more secure this idea becomes. However, a cat is also small, furry and has a tail. New environmental experience – being introduced to a cat – contradicts the currently held knowledge and understanding concerning the definition of a dog. The new information is added to the existing information, and gradually a deeper and broader understanding of creatures with fur and tails is developed.

A young child is introduced to a large white object in a kitchen and it is explained, simply, that it is hot and should not be touched. The word 'cooker' is used and remembered by the child. The child has an evolving mental structure that includes the images and ideas of a large white object in a kitchen, the word 'cooker' and the idea that it should not be touched. Very soon after this experience, the child may well walk towards the next large white object in the kitchen, actually a fridge, and call out the word 'cooker'. When corrected by the more knowledgeable adult, a problem arises. The mental model for large white objects in kitchens is incomplete and the new experience is creating a contradiction for the child. New information in the form of a simple explanation from a parent, or by observing and mentally noting differences, will add the new

---

TABLE 3.2 Piaget's assimilation and accommodation processes

- *Assimilation* is the process whereby new knowledge is incorporated into existing mental structures. The knowledge bank is increased to include new information.

- *Accommodation* is the process whereby mental structures have to be altered in order to cope with the new experience that has contradicted the existing model.

- *Equilibration* is the process of arriving at a stable state where there is no longer a conflict between new and existing knowledge.

---

information to the existing model and learning will have taken place. The unstable has been made stable and the child can move on to a future encounter with a dishwasher or a tumble-dryer.

Piaget's early work formed the basis of the constructivist learning movement. In constructivist learning theory, the key idea is that 'students actively construct their own knowledge: the mind of the student mediates input from the outside world to determine what the student will learn. Learning is active mental work, not passive reception of teaching' (Woolfolk 1993).

In constructivist learning, individuals draw on their experience of the world around them, in many different forms, and work to make sense of what they perceive in order to build an understanding of what is around them.

Within constructivist theory, there are, naturally, different interpretations of the basic ideas of the construction of knowledge and understanding. We will consider some of these interpretations; in particular, the notion of mental frameworks that hold items of knowledge in a notional, complex structure, each item having numerous links to other related items, and each link defined according to connections and interpretations constructed by the 'owner'. We will look at schema theory, which gives a model of, and an explanation for, what underpins the complex process of building new knowledge and understanding.

Schema theory

Human beings understand the world by constructing models of it in their minds.

(Johnson-Laird 1983)

Mental models, which have been described and examined by psychologists over many years (Piaget in the 1920s, Bartlett in the 1930s, Schank in the 1970s, Rumelhart in the 1980s, to mention but a few), and which form the basis of schema theory, are now fairly widely considered as a reasonable means of describing the way that the process of learning unfolds. Johnson-Laird tells us that mental models are the basic structure of cognition: 'It is now plausible to suppose that mental models play a central and unifying role in representing objects, states of affairs, sequences of events, the way the world is, and the social and psychological actions of daily life' (1983); and we are told by Holland et al. that 'mental models are the basis for all reasoning processes' (1986).

To look more closely at the idea of a schema, we can describe it as a theoretical multidimensional store for almost innumerable items of knowledge, or as a framework with numerous nodes and even more numerous connections between nodes. At each node, there is a discrete piece of information or an idea. The piece of information can be in any one of a range of different forms – image, sound, smell, feeling, action and so on. Each node is connected to many others. The connections are made as a result of there being a meaningful link between the connected items. The links are personal, and identical items in the schemas of two different people could easily have very different links made for very different reasons, which could account for individuals having a 'different understanding' of a topic or idea. It is the adding of items to schemas and connecting them to other items that constitutes constructivist learning. There is no limit to the size to which a schema might grow. There is no limit to the number of connections within a schema that might be made, and there are no restrictions on how schemas might link and interconnect with other schemas. The more connections there are within and between schemas, the more construction has taken place and the more it is considered that knowledge and understanding has been gained; that is, learning has taken place.

A schema can exist to represent a physical skill or action. An example of this might be related to handwriting: the correct way to construct a letter, the way in which spaces are created between words. A schema related to throwing a stone or a ball would be activated and then used as a basis for learning how to throw a javelin. The stone-throwing schema would not be directly or fully applicable in the case where a longer, heavier object to throw was to be used, where there are significant differences in style and posture required to be successful. However, a child with a well-developed schema related to throwing a ball or similar object would be able to develop it into a successful schema to use in a variety of 'throwing' situations.

Figure 3.1 (based on Davis 1991) is an attempt to represent a schema, though it must be understood that to draw a schema is essentially impossible. This representation is limited by many factors, space being one. The notional 'egg' schema would have numerous links to other schemas, and in itself constitute a tiny subset (or subschema) of a more expansive structure. This particular restricted schema would form only a very tiny proportion of the whole knowledge base of an individual.

In some respects, a schema might be looked upon as a framework of reference. When a new phenomenon is encountered, whether it be a new word that is similar in some way to a word that already 'known', or a new item of food, it is compared to a schema that already exists and comparisons are made. Similarities and differences are discerned; we might say, or think perhaps, 'It's a bit like . . .' or 'It reminds me of . . .'. These considerations are indicative of a schema being referenced and used as a tool for understanding or prediction.

Characteristics of schemas include:

- They are based on our general world knowledge and experiences.
- They are generalised knowledge about situations, objects, events, feelings and actions.
- They are incomplete and constantly evolving.
- They are personal.
- They are not usually totally accurate representations of a phenomenon.
- They typically contain inaccuracies and contradictions (misconceptions).
- They provide simplified explanations of complex phenomena.
- They contain uncertainty, but are used even if incorrect.

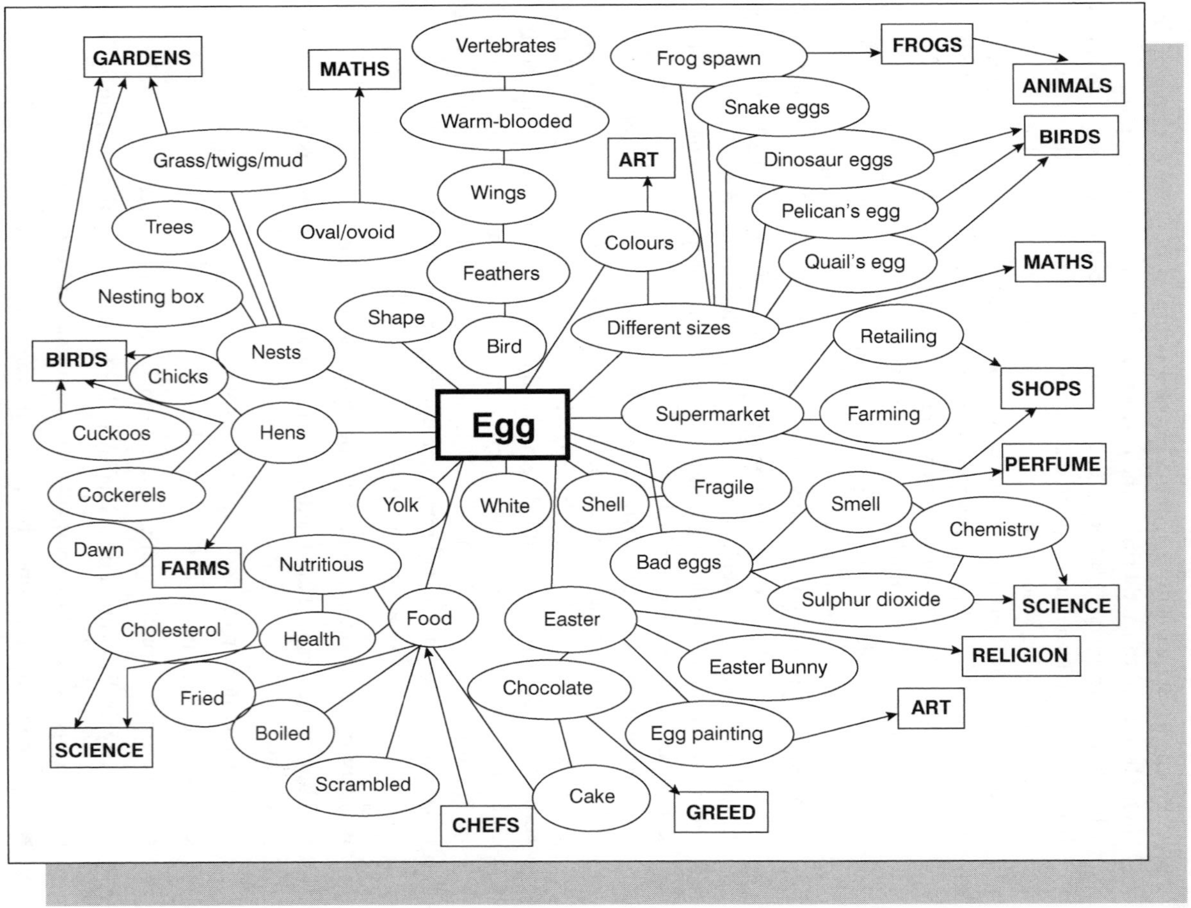

Figure 3.1
Egg schema diagram (Davis 1991)

- They guide our understanding of new information by providing explanations of what is happening, what it means and what is likely to result.

Prior knowledge has a crucial part to play in constructivist learning. An existing schema represents the sum of an individual's current state of knowledge and understanding of the particular topic, event, action and so on. New learning concerned with the particular topic will involve the processes of accommodation and assimilation, and the expansion and increase in complexity of the schema in question. For this reason, it is very important that a schema that is to be the focus of these processes in the introduction of a new area of work in school is activated at the outset of a new topic, and reactivated each time the learning is to move on in subsequent lessons. In simple terms, if new learning is to take place, it is a very good idea to review what is already known about the topic in question. The starting point of what is already known and understood is very important if any new learning is to be effective. Schema activation is a process that can be encouraged in classroom situations, and teachers frequently make use of this idea in their work.

Schema theory: a summary

Cognitive psychologists refer to units of knowledge, understanding and skill as schemas, as a way of referring to conceptual knowledge that is stored in long-term memory. It is estimated that any adult would have hundreds of thousands of schemas in memory that would be interrelated in an extremely large and complex number of different ways. New schemas are being created constantly, and existing schemas are updated with equal regularity. This creating and updating takes place every time that we read, listen to, observe, try out, or sense in any other way anything new. New schemas are created every time that one fact is linked to another by a logical or semantic connection. Each schema is a subschema of another larger and related schema, and each schema has a set of subschemas of its own – this is an image of a very complex network, each schema with a variety of links and relationships with a great number of others. Schemas are used as a point of reference when new phenomena are encountered.

Mayer (1983) lists four elements that describe a schema:

1 *General:* a schema may be used in a wide variety of situations as a framework for understanding incoming information.
2 *Knowledge:* a schema exists in memory as something that a person knows.
3 *Structure:* a schema is organised around some theme.
4 *Comprehension:* a schema contains slots that are filled in by specific information.

Social constructivism

The origins of the constructivist view of learning have their roots in the work of Piaget. Piaget viewed the growing child as a 'lone scientist'; that is, one who works, experiments and makes discoveries on their own. (This notion of child as 'scientist' is referenced by more recent writers, such as Karmiloff-Smith (1992) and Gopnik and Meltzoff (1997), but the notion of them being alone in their endeavours is no longer seen as the full picture, as we will see.) This description gives an image of a child alone, exploring the immediate environment and drawing conclusions about the nature and structure of the world. Social constructivism adds an important dimension to the constructivist domain. In social constructivist theory, emphasis is placed upon interaction between the learner and others. The others can come in many forms – it is the dimension of social interaction that is crucial to the social constructivists. The main proponents of this branch of constructivism are Lev Vygotsky (1896–1934), a Russian psychologist whose work was carried out at the start of the twentieth century, but not widely available in the West until many years later, and Jerome Bruner (born in 1915), an American psychologist publishing his work in the second half of the twentieth century.

Social constructivism gives a high priority to language in the process of intellectual development. Dialogue becomes the vehicle by which ideas are considered, shared and developed. The dialogue is often with a more knowledgeable other, but this need not always be the case. Dialogue with peers can be of equal value. Prior knowledge, naturally, has a part to play. It is an individual's prior and current knowledge that forms the basis of any contribution to a dialogue. It is with reference to existing knowledge and understanding (schemas) that new ideas and understanding can be constructed in the course of dialogue. When we consider the more knowledgeable other, it is easy to assume that this person will be a teacher or a parent, but this need not be the case. More knowledgeable need not imply older, nor need it imply being in a position of responsibility for learning; this is something often overlooked when considering the notional 'teacher–pupil' relationship. It is perfectly possible for the role of 'teacher', especially in casual, informal situations, to be taken by a peer, a casual acquaintance, a younger sibling and so on. It is very often the case that learning will take place in very different environments. Most learning does not take place in school. Any social interaction with anybody at all may well lead to learning. The building and exchange of thoughts and ideas that takes place in the course of a discussion, in any context at all, is likely for at least one of the participants, and often for both or all of them, to lead to a greater understanding of, or insight into, the topic of the conversation.

Scaffolding

The role of the more knowledgeable other in formal learning situations is usually taken by a teacher. The teacher has the role of stimulating dialogue and maintaining its momentum. In a very real way, the teacher engages groups and individuals in dialogue and supports the development of understanding. The undertaking of this role, in a planned way, is known as 'scaffolding'. To fully understand the concept of scaffolding, we need to first look at an aspect of Vygotsky's work, which is the notion of a zone of proximal development (or ZPD).

The zone of proximal development is a refreshingly simple description of something that many teachers and other adults understand and work with. It is an idea from Vygotsky's work that has impacted on practice over the last 20 years or so, as more importance has been given to the notion of differentiation in teaching.

The zone of proximal development is a theoretical space of understanding that is just above the level of understanding of a given individual. It is the area of understanding into which a learner will move next. In the zone of proximal development, a learner is able to work effectively, but only with support. The zone is necessarily different for each individual child. The process of learning involves moving into and across the zone and looking forward to the next level of understanding, or ability, which will involve a similar journey through a newly created zone. Sewell (1990) explains it as 'a point at which a child has partly mastered a skill, but can act more effectively with the assistance of a more skilled adult or peer'.

Passing through the zone of proximal development is a process that can be aided by the intervention of another. A teacher can fulfil this role, and so can a range of other people or materials. In planning work for children, a teacher needs to take into account the current state of the understanding of the children in question, and plan accordingly and appropriately.

Scaffolding is the process of giving support to learners at the appropriate time and at the appropriate level of sophistication to meet the needs of the individual. Scaffolding can be presented in many ways: through discussion – a good socially constructive approach; through the provision of materials – perhaps supplying practical apparatus to help in the solution of simple problems in arithmetic; or by designing tasks that match, and give help appropriate to, the individual – a list of words given to help in the process of completing an exercise designed to assist understanding, or a list of reminders concerning the process of undertaking the task in question; a writing frame to support a particular style of written piece is also an example.

Working collaboratively, in pairs or small groups, is an obvious socially constructive approach to learning. The converse of this would be working in a silent classroom, where contact with others is discouraged. There are times when quiet individual working is useful and important, and teachers are able to describe times when a child should be encouraged to work quietly and alone. As a mainstay approach to teaching and learning, however, this would totally ignore all that we know about socially constructed learning.

Situated learning and authentic activity

'Situated learning' refers to the fact that all learning takes place in a context. The context may or may not be familiar to the learner. If the context is unfamiliar – or, perhaps, not very familiar – to the learner, learning will not necessarily proceed smoothly.

Situated learning (Lave and Wenger 1991), in part, suggests that skills, knowledge and understanding that are learnt, and even mastered, in one context may not necessarily be transferred successfully to another. Another aspect of situated learning, which is more relevant here, is the notion that learning can be situated in social and cultural settings, and that, if a learning activity falls beyond the cultural understanding of the learner, then learning is likely, at best, to be less successful than if it had been situated in a more familiar setting. For example, giving young children the task of investigating the pros and cons of fox hunting when their cultural setting is a deprived inner-city area where contact with the countryside, with animals, domestic or wild, and the emotions associated with the discovery of ravaged lambs or roosting hens are alien to them, is very unlikely, without exceptionally detailed and sympathetic introductions and the provision of first-hand experience, to lead to good quality learning experiences. In order to introduce the children to the ideas of making a case, and arguing for particular points of view, it would be far more reasonable to invite them to consider something within their cultural domain. The same would almost certainly be true in reverse: children brought up in a rural environment with little experience of city life might well find it difficult to understand, and learn from, notions concerning overcrowded housing estates and parents fearful of letting their children play and roam freely.

There is a link between the idea of learning being situated and the need for authentic learning tasks. Much has been written on this matter (see, for example, McFarlane 1997). Authentic tasks are 'tasks that pupils can relate to their own experience inside and outside school; tasks that an experienced practitioner would undertake' (Selinger 2001). When learning is made up of authentic tasks, there is a greater probability of engagement with the task and also with the information and ideas involved with the task. Authentic tasks are likely to hold the attention and interest of the children and lead to a deeper level of engagement than with another similar, but 'non-authentic', or, at least, less authentic task. This links closely with the ideas put forward by the sociocultural learning theorists. Bruner (1996), Brown *et al.* (1989) and others support the need for culturally linked and authentic learning tasks. This has the desirable effect of making the difference between learning in school and 'out-of-school learning' less well defined. Children working with new ideas in a familiar context are far more likely to engage with the ideas than if the same ideas are presented in an alien context.

Social learning theory

Social learning theory emphasises the role of observation and participation as a means of learning. Interaction with others is stressed, but it is not seen as fundamental to learning in the way that it is in social constructivism (Pritchard and

Woollard, 2010). Bandura's theory (1977) is linked closely to Piaget's earlier work. As a constructivist thinker, he considers learning as an active process. However, in contrast to Piaget, he stresses the importance of the social nature of learning. Bandura's theory is fully consistent with social constructivist thought. He shows that human lives are not lived in isolation (Royer 2005), and describes what he calls 'collective agency', which is an extension of the more individualised 'human agency'. Collective agency is concerned with people working together on shared beliefs and with common aspirations to improve their lives. Bandura argues that people learn from observing role models in day-to-day life, explaining that: 'Learning would be exceedingly laborious, not to mention hazardous, if people had to rely solely on the effects of their own actions to inform them what to do.' (1977)

This notion of observational learning links with the concept of 'situativity', which is at the heart of the theory of situated learning that we have considered above. Situated learning, and what is referred to as the apprenticeship model, refers to learning taking place in social situations. 'Social', in this sense, refers to a situation in which two or more individuals are together and interacting at some level in a way that encourages learning to take place for one or more of those present. The label 'apprenticeship' is used as a reference to the traditional relationship between a master craftsperson and an apprentice, a traditional model of training and learning in many of the craft occupations. The apprentice can be seen to be 'looking and learning', which is an example of Bandura's observational learning. The apprentice is tutored by example and guided in their efforts by the highly skilled master. In this model, learning proceeds by demonstration and instruction, followed by emulation and repeated practice. By proximity to the master and through a process of social engagement, it is expected that the apprentice will acquire the skills of the trade. Another idea from this area of theory is that of 'legitimate peripheral participation'. In a social group, where it is expected that the younger members of the group will learn the skills and acquire the knowledge that is commonly held within the group, the learner is said to be a legitimate participant, and the fact that the learner is not a central member of the group makes him or her peripheral. An example of this learning process can be seen in the way that younger children might learn the skills and rules of a game by joining in with older children who have already mastered the skills and rules of the game in question.

Metacognition

'Cognition' is a global term that seeks to cover all of the mental activities that serve the acquisition, storage, retrieval and use of knowledge. Cognition is the ability of the brain to think, to process and store information and to solve problems. Cognition is a high-level behaviour that is thought, in many respects, to be unique to humans. Piaget considered that it was the ability to engage in abstract thought, which is a high-level cognitive activity, that set human cognition apart from the cognition of all other creatures (see earlier in this chapter). Some would take issue with this, pointing to recent work with apes who have exhibited outstanding feats of cognitive endeavour, but, for our purposes, we need to be satisfied with looking at human cognition alone. Obviously, the role of cognition in the processes of learning is crucial. 'Metacognition' refers to the idea of an individual's considering, being aware of and understanding their own mental (cognitive) processes and ways of learning. It is cognition about cognition. An individual's awareness of their own thought processes will have a bearing on the way that they view their own learning, and is likely, with encouragement, to lead to recognition of the ways in which they might learn most effectively.

Metacognition: a definition

Metacognitive knowledge is the knowledge that an individual has about their own cognition, which can be used to consider and to control their cognitive processes. To work metacognitively is to consider and take active control of the processes involved in learning and thinking as they are happening.

The term 'metacognition' is most closely associated with the psychologist John Flavell (1976; 1977). He tells us that metacognition consists of metacognitive knowledge and metacognitive experiences or regulation. Metacognitive knowledge is knowledge about cognitive processes that an individual has come to understand, and that can be used to control mental processes. 'Metacognition refers to one's knowledge concerning one's cognitive processes and products or anything related to them [. . .] metacognition refers, among other things, to the active monitoring [. . .] regulation and orchestration of these processes' (Flavell 1976). Brown (1987) offers a simpler version of this when he says that 'Metacognition refers loosely to one's knowledge and control of [one's] own cognitive system.'

An example of an approach to learning spellings that is influenced by ideas from metacognition involves talking explicitly about how to learn them. In the past, at least in the experience of many of us, teachers have been known to give the instruction: 'Write down these spellings and learn them for a test next week.' This is all well and good for some children, but for others it represents an insurmountable problem – how do they learn them? We all have very different approaches to tasks of this type, and some children will find a way that helps them to learn lists of spellings, but many others will not. If attention is drawn to the fact that there are ways of approaching such a task and that different individuals may find different approaches more suitable, then the door has been opened to the world of developing strategies for accomplishing particular desired outcomes. This is an example of metacognitive awareness. One child may say something like this: 'I just photograph it and then I know it.' Another may say that they can only learn the spellings by repeatedly saying them aloud to a parent. Another might talk about writing and rewriting the list; yet another might well say that they have no approach and are at a loss when it comes to attempting to learn them. As teachers, we cannot say which strategy will suit which child, but we can provide opportunities for a group to pool ideas and discuss them. Then, children can be encouraged to experiment with different approaches. One tried and reasonably successful approach to learning spellings or foreign language vocabulary is the 'look–say–cover–write–check' method. This involves mental activity and the necessity to hold a spelling in short-term memory as well as immediate feedback being provided. Once introduced, this method may or may not suit a particular child. It is hoped that exposure to this method, and discussion of its purpose and value, at the same time as considering possible alternatives, will allow children to decide, in a metacognitive mode, how to approach the task in question.

In a related example, sometimes children are completely lost when it comes to undertaking simple mental calculation. Individual approaches to mental calculation vary widely, and some approaches seem complicated and difficult to one person, but clear and simple to another. The Cockcroft report (1982) found that the ways in which adults undertook mental arithmetic tasks varied enormously, and that idiosyncratic approaches were very widespread. This is wholly acceptable if arriving at the correct answer is the prime objective, but, for young children trying to find their way with mental calculation, some insight into their own approaches and processes is very important. This insight into how to think in what are, for some, difficult abstract terms is metacognitive, and very helpful in the process of learning how to undertake the task in question. Teachers can encourage approaches to develop metacognitive awareness in simple ways; for example, by asking children to describe their own approaches, and by giving value to the identification of the methods and processes followed by different individuals. Instead of being satisfied with a correct answer, a teacher can probe below the surface to discover the approach taken. This is also helpful when incorrect responses to mental calculation are given. The process of sharing and experimenting with different approaches to carrying out mental calculations in an environment that is safe and supportive can, in a socially constructive way, lead to individuals developing both a fuller understanding of their own processes of thinking and, in this case, an understanding of how to tackle particular tasks.

A consideration of which approaches best suit an individual can be of immense value at times of 'routine' learning – such times as learning spellings, practising methods in maths or other factual content that needs to be internalised – but it is possibly more valuable when revision is undertaken for exams. Knowing how to best approach learning of this type can be considered by teachers and it is important to encourage learners, at every level, to discover how they learn and what suits them individually.

Wray and Lewis (1997) single out four aspects of constructivist learning theory that they consider to be of paramount importance:

1 Learning is a process of interaction between what is known and what is to be learnt.

2 Learning is a social process.

3 Learning is a situated process.

4 Learning is a metacognitive process.

From these four aspects of constructivist theory, they go on to formulate four principles for teaching:

1 Learners need enough previous knowledge and understanding to enable them to learn new things; they need help making explicit the links with new and previous knowledge.

2 Provision should be made for social interaction and discussion in groups of varying sizes, both with and without the teacher.

3 Meaningful contexts for learning are very important; it must be remembered that what is meaningful for a teacher is not necessarily meaningful for the child.

4 Children's awareness of their own thought processes should be promoted.

All of what has gone before in this chapter points, more or less, to what should be a very important element of learning: that is, mental activity. Mental activity should be at the centre of our teaching methods, and can be encouraged in a variety of ways. When dealing with new experiences, learning seems to proceed well if the points above are in place *and* if there is mental activity on the part of the learner.

Mental activity

Learning is not something that others can undertake on behalf of learners. It is something that learners must do for themselves. Adults – whether teachers, trainers or parents – cannot assume that, if they exert thought and effort, directed towards teaching, then learning will be the inevitable result. Learning requires effort on the part of the learner, and, without some effort and some mental activity, it is very unlikely that learning will take place. In the context of constructivist theory, learning is an active, not a passive, activity. Teachers continually put into place situations in which learning is likely, but without the required effort and activity on the part of the would-be learner, the outcome is not at all certain. Howe (1999) tells us that:

Learning always necessitates mental activities being undertaken by the individual learner [. . .] Learning does not always have to be deliberate, but it does always require the engagement of mental processes. The mental activities of individual students form a particularly powerful source of influence on what is actually learned.

We are also told that: 'The role of the teacher is to recognise the importance of mental activity in learning' (Chastain 1971).

Engagement

Everything about the constructivist approach to learning, in a simple and practical way, points towards the importance of learners getting as close to the material content of what it is hoped they will learn as possible and then 'doing' something with it. By undertaking actions and activities, mental or physical, that centre on the facts, the concepts or the skills in question, learners are in a position to move forward in their learning. This 'closeness' is possible in a wide range of different ways, and is sometimes referred to as 'engagement'.

For children to understand new information, they must become actively involved with it; that is, they need to engage with it. There is a five-stage model for learning, put forward by a group of Australian teachers and academics, which puts engagement at the start of the process of learning; which takes a wholly constructivist approach; and within which the importance of the individual and of activity are stressed. As we have seen, from the constructivist point of view, learning is not a passive process, and so, with reference to what is known about effective learning, and with due attention paid to the notion of engagement, it is possible to map out approaches to learning that encompass the best and most effective of what is currently known about learning.

The five-stage model (Reid *et al.* 1989) sets out a route that, if followed, is likely to provide the conditions required for learning to result:

1 engagement

2 exploration

3 transformation

4 presentation

5 reflection.

'Engagement' is described as 'the time during which students acquire information and engage in an experience that provides the basis for, or content of, their ensuing learning' (Reid *et al.* 1989). The next stage in the model – 'exploration' – is closely related to the stage of engagement. This stage can be an open-ended process, where children follow their instincts, but possibly a more profitable approach for teachers to take with their classes is to set short tasks that develop both engagement and exploration. These tasks are designed to give the child an overview of what is contained in the information under consideration, and may take many forms, including reading and writing tasks; finding things out and answering questions; more manipulative activities; matching and comparing; drawing or compiling charts or diagrams; discussing and arguing, in pairs or in groups; and many other diverse and related tasks.

'Transformation' is the stage in which information with which the child has engaged, and has explored, might be reconfigured into a form that allows for 'presentation' (the next stage), but, importantly, transformed into a format that will, from the teacher's point of view, enable learning objectives to be met. From the point of view of the child, certain questions will now be able to be answered.

Transformation and the resultant presentation is not the end of the process. Time to reflect upon what has been undertaken, the process and the content, gives the opportunity for internalisation, and for a deeper level of understanding to be developed. 'Reflection' can also take many forms. One common approach is to ask children to give a short presentation/explanation of what they have been doing and what they have learnt. This can take a variety of different formats, prepared for a variety of different audiences – a poster to display, a newspaper front page, a multimedia presentation, or something as simple as a 30-second explanation of what they have been doing in the lesson, possibly including what they have learnt. This idea has become a part of the plenary session that now forms an integral part of many lessons in British schools.

Bereiter and Scardamalia (1987) describe a model of the writing process that they term 'knowledge transformation'. Knowledge transformation can be seen as the reshaping or reconstruction of information in order to answer certain questions, to help meet particular learning objectives and to assist the learner in the process of coming to understand the content of their learning activity. This model is characterised by the writer alone accomplishing what is normally accomplished through the medium of social dialogue. Knowledge is considered and 'worked upon' by the individual – engagement takes place. This dialogue, which forms an important element of the thinking that underpins social constructivism, is seen as the medium through which learning takes place. A child working alone cannot take part in an actual dialogue, which has the possibility of allowing engagement with the knowledge and ideas of the topic in question, but, by undertaking a process of knowledge transformation, a similar process may come into play and effective learning may be possible.

Encouraging engagement

We have seen that without engagement with the content of an activity, effective learning is far less likely to be the result of anything that teachers ask children to do. It can be surmised that an important element of the role of the teacher is to encourage engagement, since, without some measure of involvement with information and ideas and the undertaking of activity centred on the content (Bereiter and Scardamalia's knowledge transformation, for example), there is a greatly reduced opportunity for effective learning to take place, especially the deep learning that is the aim of most teaching situations.

There are many effective ways of encouraging children to engage with their work. Taking into account the prior knowledge of the children, the level of difficulty, the social and cultural context and the general level of interest of the subject matter will all help with the need for engagement.

Certain guidelines can apply to the planning of lessons, such as that lessons need:

- a clear focus and goals, with explicit learning objectives;
- to be based upon the pupils' existing knowledge;
- to be set in an appropriate context;
- to include scope for social interaction and for activity;
- to be planned in such a way that they aim to move the pupils' learning forward (across the zone of proximal development).

The points above can all be traced back to what is known about the way that we learn, and to the work of many psychologists and educationalists in the field of learning. It would be unrealistic to suggest that, if all of the above were in place, then effective learning is certain to result, since, as all teachers know, there are a great many variables – some of which are controllable and others that are not – that can so easily influence the outcome of any particular lesson. However, taking into account what is known about learning, and about how children learn, will increase the possibility of effective learning resulting from the activity undertaken.

Summary

Cognitivist definition of learning

Learning is a relatively permanent change in mental associations as a result of experience. The changes in mental associations are internal and cannot easily be observed.

Mental activity

The importance of mental activity (engagement) for effective learning is at the heart of the way that cognitive psychologists describe and understand the process of learning.

Essential features of constructivism

Constructivist learning theory is built around a set of important features that can be summed up as follows (after Jonassen *et al.* 1999):

The construction of knowledge and not the reproduction of knowledge is paramount

It is the processes that the learner puts into place and uses that are important, rather than the fact of knowing something as an end product. A learner is actively engaged with, and in control of, the learning process.

Learning can lead to multiple representations of reality

When learning involves the use of a variety of resources (e.g. first-hand experience, secondary sources, interactive materials, independent research, dialogue), alternative viewpoints of the subject in question are formed; this, in turn, can be used to foster the skills of critical thinking.

Authentic tasks in a meaningful context are encouraged

Authentic tasks, such as problem solving, are used to situate learning in familiar and realistic contexts.

Reflection on prior experience is encouraged

Learners are prompted to relate new knowledge and concepts to pre-existing knowledge and experience, which allows the 'new' to integrate with what is known already, and, in this way, adding to a learner's framework of understanding (schema) or amending it.

Collaborative work for learning is encouraged

Dialogue with others allows additional and alternative perspectives to be taken into account when developing personal conclusions. Different knowledge, points of view and understanding can be given and considered before moving on.

Autonomy in learning is encouraged

Learners are given, and accept, increasing amounts of responsibility for their own learning. This happens in a number of different ways: by collaborating with others, by working on self-generated problems and by the formulating of, and testing of, hypotheses, for example.

The appendix of this book includes a summary chart of the differences and similarities between the work of Piaget and Vygotsky.

In the classroom

- Opportunities for mental activity are essential; this leads to deeper engagement with ideas and increases the possibility of effective, lasting learning taking place.
- Social interaction – that is, discussion between pairs, groups and between teacher and pupils – is essential for the effective development of understanding.
- Learning set in meaningful contexts is far more likely to engage learners than if it is set in other, random or remote contexts. Make learning meaningful by placing it in a setting with which children can identify. For example, when

teaching about time, refer to the fixed points in the school day, bedtimes or the length of football matches. This may appear trivial, but it can make a big difference.

- Encourage learners to review what they know about a new topic before embarking on new teaching. Ask questions. Remind the class of work from the previous term or year.

- Encourage learners, with appropriate guidance, to find things out for themselves.

- Gauge the processes of teacher intervention carefully so as to encourage thought processes. Telling is not teaching, but measured scaffolding is.

- Encourage learners to think about and put into words the methods or approaches that they use in the course of their work – how they undertake mental arithmetic, for example, or consider how to prepare for a test.

- Allow time for learners to reflect upon what they have learnt. Well-managed plenaries at the end of lessons are very good for this.

4

Multiple intelligences

Howard Gardner's multiple intelligence theory (Gardner 1983; 1993) proposes the idea that we all have various levels of intelligence across a range of intellectual areas. Gardner's theory comes, in part, out of a concern that when intelligence is measured, the most commonly used tests (standard verbal and non-verbal reasoning tests) often do not allow those tested to demonstrate what they are really good at or where their intelligence lies. Gardner gives us a set of different 'intelligences' that, as individuals, we display more or less of, according to our particular intellectual make-up. There are nine of these intelligences, but Gardner does not rule out the defining of others. Currently, they are:

1 *linguistic*: enjoyment of and facility with reading, poetry and all things literary and linguistic;

2 *logical/mathematical*: enjoyment of and facility with maths and science, games of strategy and any logic-based pursuits;

3 *musical*: enjoyment of and facility with music – listening, playing and perhaps composing;

4 *spatial/visual*: enjoyment of and facility with images, drawing, construction games and tactile puzzles such as jigsaws;

5 *kinaesthetic*: enjoyment of and facility with activities that involve touch and movement, dance, sport and other practical activities;

6 *interpersonal*: enjoyment of and facility with other people, communication, leadership and the ability to empathise;

7 *intrapersonal*: enjoyment of and facility with self-motivation, no dependence on others, awareness of one's own feelings more than those of others – often seen as shyness;

8 *naturalistic*: enjoyment of and facility with the natural world, with ability in recognising patterns and classification;

9 *existential*: enjoyment of and facility with asking and examining questions about life, death and ultimate realities.

Originally, Gardner described only seven intelligences, though later he established an eighth and a ninth. Also under consideration as possible human intelligences are 'spiritual' and 'moral', though these are considered somewhat problematic.

An individual's particular strengths in intelligences have a direct bearing upon the way in which their learning takes place. For example, someone with interpersonal strengths would be most likely to learn effectively in a social situation where relating ideas and knowledge to others can be encouraged. The opposite might be true for an individual with low interpersonal intelligence but a strength in intrapersonal intelligence.

To be aware of multiple intelligence strengths and our preferred or most effective learning approach is to be operating at a metacognitive level, as we saw in Chapter 3.

Multiple intelligences in the classroom

If the ideas set out by Gardner are to be taken seriously, then there are ramifications for the ways in which teachers teach and for the types of activities in which children in school are expected to take part. For example, a child with particular strengths that are not in the linguistic domain might well be disadvantaged if, without exception, the work that is expected of him or her relies heavily on being able to express ideas through words. This can also be true for children with other specific multiple intelligence strengths that are not catered for, in some way, in their lessons.

There are many examples of the sort of problems that might occur when the majority of responses to schoolwork rely on the abilities of the children to function effectively in the domains associated with one or other of the intelligences. Those with strengths in interpersonal intelligence who are expected to work in a solitary fashion; those who have kinaesthetic strengths and aptitudes and are not 'allowed' to work practically or to move around; and those with intrapersonal strengths and preferences who are required to operate as a part of a group working collaboratively to solve a problem are just three examples of the ways in which an ignorance of – or disregard for – individual 'intelligence', in Gardner's terms, can lead to disadvantage.

In planning for multiple intelligences, teachers consider the range of activities related to the content of the lesson and the intended learning outcomes that will give a range of opportunities to the children's different intelligence strengths. This can be approached by seeking to answer certain questions, such as:

- *Logical/mathematical*: How can I include the use of numbers, classification, critical thinking and calculations?
- *Spatial*: How can I include pictures and diagrams, colours, art or graphs?
- *Intrapersonal*: How can I include private learning time and choice?
- *Interpersonal*: How can I include group work, peer sharing and discussions?

- *Kinaesthetic*: How can I include movement, practical apparatus, drama or art and craft?

- *Musical*: How can I include music, sounds, rhyme, rhythms and dance?

- *Linguistic*: How can I include reading, writing and speaking? (Gigglepotz 2000).

It may not be possible for each and every lesson to have appropriate answers for all of the questions above, but, over a period of time, the planning process would allow for a balanced and, in terms of the perceived needs of the children, an equitable and suitable 'multiple intelligence friendly' set of classroom activities for learning.

A part of the approach taken in learning situations planned around multiple intelligences involves allowing for a wide variety of responses to particular tasks. In many school learning situations, the standard response to the investigation of a new learning topic is to write about it in a standard, almost formulaic way. In a multiple intelligence environment, set responses are not required. Often, a range of different responses are encouraged, and, at the least, a choice between a number of ways of recording work or other ways of dealing with new knowledge and ideas are given. The example below, from an American school, illustrates this point:

> Three eight- and nine-year-old boys recently gave an oral report about California to their classmates. The students sang and danced [to] an original song about the state, played a short video they produced, displayed maps drawn to scale and spiritedly presented a series of facts. Are these students academically advanced or exceptionally creative? No, such multi-modal learning is commonplace in a third-/fourth-/fifth-grade multi-aged classroom at Cascade Elementary School in Maryville, WA.
>
> (Campbell and Campbell 1993)

In the description of the classroom organisation and approach to teaching employed in the classroom in the example above, we are told of different learning centres around the room where all children, in groups of three or four, spend time each day working on the topic of the day. This is a setting where the importance of the notion of multiple intelligences has been given high priority and where what might be considered a traditional approach to classroom organisation has been set aside in favour of a new approach. The article continues to describe a year-long action research project that set out to test the approach. The results, as reported, seem good, with gains noted across a range of measures, including the demonstration of increased responsibility, self-direction and independence; a significant reduction in discipline problems; improved co-operative learning; and improvement in academic achievement, measured by comparisons in grades achieved in standardised tests.

In the context of a more traditional setting, it is still possible for teachers to take multiple intelligences into account and to allow for a variety of responses to work that is to be covered. Some teachers allow for this by giving an element of choice in the way that work is recorded; for example, a written piece, a pictorial/diagrammatic piece or an audio-recording of a news item. This approach encapsulates both the notion that learners have different multiple intelligence strengths and also, as we will see in Chapter 5, that individual learners have preferred learning styles. These two areas of theory are closely related.

One approach to dealing with addressing multiple intelligences is to proceed in the usual way with planning and teaching, but to also plan for a range of follow-up activities, each set in the domain of a different intelligence. This is exemplified by Tom Hoerr in *Celebrating Multiple Intelligences: Teaching for Success* (1996). A lesson based on the Eric Carle book *The Very Hungry Caterpillar* ([1969] 2002) is described and a set of follow-up activities are presented, each of which would appeal to children with different multiple intelligence strengths. The introductory section of the lesson, where the story is read and shared with the class, is, in itself, creative and interesting, and the options for following up are diverse and give ample opportunity for individuals to work in a manner suited to their particular multiple intelligence situation.

The introduction to the lesson was creative and fun, but, in many ways, no different from the ways in which many teachers might choose to introduce a story and share the experience and fun of reading a story with the class. As the story, which is generally well known, relates the experiences of a caterpillar that eventually transforms into a butterfly, the teacher produced a puppet caterpillar, made from a sock, and inside hid a felt model of the butterfly. At the appropriate stage, the sock puppet was removed to expose the unfolding butterfly.

The story was discussed in detail, and the sequence, in particular, given special attention. Additional pictures of real caterpillars and butterflies were introduced and discussed. The children were able to relate some of their experiences concerning the story. The teacher led a discussion about the characteristics of caterpillars and butterflies, and a list of descriptive words was generated.

The story, and the added impact of the use of puppets, held the attention and interest of the class, as we would normally expect. It is in the style of activities that were presented next that the importance of individual multiple intelligence strengths is taken into account.

Follow-up activities

- *Interpersonal*: Working in small groups, produce posters that illustrate the metamorphosis in the story.
- *Intrapersonal*: Discuss how it might feel to change from a caterpillar to a butterfly. This could be an actual discussion or a written piece.
- *Kinaesthetic*: Act out the stages of metamorphosis.
- *Logical/mathematical*: Count how many times each fruit appears in the book. Make a chart of the fruits and examine the relationship between the numbers.

- *Musical*: Crawl like caterpillars and fly like butterflies to fast/slow music.
- *Spatial*: Children make their own sock caterpillars.

Clearly, the organisation of the activities could become complex, and there is a need for the teacher to take control to ensure that the activities are well supported and that appropriate numbers of children are directed towards certain activities at certain times. The 'kinaesthetic' activity, for example, might well be best suited to a time when the school hall is available for PE time, but there is always the option of allowing a group to work on this at other times. The same might apply to the 'musical' activity. The making of sock puppets could be reserved for an art lesson, or, again, this could be offered as an activity to choose at an appropriate time.

Working in the way described above may well ring some alarm bells for teachers, who might assume that individual children could be in a position whereby they are given choice and where they always choose a particular style of follow-up activity and choose to avoid others – writing, for example. This is where the careful monitoring that teachers engage in becomes increasingly important. Certainly, children need to be able to express themselves in the ways in which they are most expert and most comfortable, but this should not be at the expense of work in other important areas of the curriculum.

The Theory into Practice database and website (Kearsley [n.d.]), which features overviews of many aspects of learning theory, suggests three principles that, if the ideas of multiple intelligences are to be taken seriously, should be applied in school. They are:

1 Individuals should be encouraged to use their preferred intelligences in learning.

2 Instructional activities should appeal to different forms of intelligence.

3 Assessment of learning should measure multiple forms of intelligence.

In order to apply these principles, schools would have to radically rethink many of the established processes and principles that are currently in place. For many teachers, this would present great difficulty. In schools where the established approach to teaching and learning is in some way fixed and not open to individual interpretation by individual teachers, for individual teachers to apply aspects of practice founded on Gardner's theory would be very difficult. However, to take Gardner's work into account at a less radical level is something that many teachers can do and are doing. Small changes – or, at least, a measure of variety – in the ways in which children are asked to work are noticeable in many situations. Recently, a secondary school in the UK, following in-service training dealing with the notions of multiple intelligences, trialled a series of different approaches to work set by teachers. In the history department, for example, when learning about the time of the First World War, the class was given a set of options concerning the ways in which they would submit work for assessment. The options included:

- creating a three-dimensional model;
- creating a set of posters;
- filming a short drama;
- using PowerPoint software to present questions and answers;
- audio-recording a series of radio documentary articles.

The option to work alone, in a pair or in a larger group was also given. The possibility of presenting the end product to the class in the form of a formal presentation – a short talk, for example, or an annotated display – was also given. In themselves, these options for producing an end product are not unusual, but the element of choice, which allows individuals to follow their strengths, interests or even instincts, is, for many teachers, an innovation. Choice has, for some teachers, presented a challenge. Some teachers, at times, shy away from it. In many cases, there is evidence that the level of engagement with an activity, and the quality of the work produced as a result, is very high – indeed, much higher than might have been expected – when choice has been allowed. The assessment of such varied end products will clearly present challenges, but not of such magnitude that they are insurmountable.

Johnson and Kuntz (1997) carried out a study of the ways in which teachers who had attended a variety of different styles of training in the use of the multiple intelligences approach responded to the ideas to which they had been intro-duced, once they returned to their schools. They found that, overall, those surveyed believed they were applying the theory in their classrooms in ways that made a significant, positive impact upon teaching and learning. They found that:

1 Multiple intelligences were used as a basis for change in their classrooms in a variety of ways:
   - *Planning*: Teachers reported that they had begun to plan for teaching in ways that use as many intelligences as possible.
   - *General teaching*: All teachers reported that they began to involve more intelligences in teaching.
   - *Individualised teaching*: Teachers had begun to tailor teaching according to the intelligence profiles of their individual children. One teacher commented: 'Teaching must change to meet the different learning styles and strengths of my class.'
   - *Self-assessment*: Teachers considered it important to teach the class about multiple intelligence theory, and encouraged them to assess and become aware of their own intelligences profile.
   - *Assessment*: Teachers' views on assessment changed. One teacher said that: 'The most significant realisation I've had is that children can be assessed in many different ways.' Children were given more choice in how their learning was measured, and assessment became an ongoing and integrated part of teaching.

2 Diversity in learning is appreciated:

- *Teacher awareness*: Having been introduced to multiple intelligences, teachers were able to develop a better appreciation of the various skills of children in their class. One teacher confirmed this by saying: 'It has just brought home the fact that we are all diverse learners, and it [the application of multiple intelligence theory in teaching] is a way that I can address that diversity.'
- *Success*: An appreciation of diversity apparently began to contribute to greater involvement and more success for more children.

3 Classroom climate is more positive:

- *Co-operative*: The climate becomes more co-operative as children come to understand and gain more respect for one another's strengths.
- *Engaged*: Many teachers find that multiple intelligences-based approaches 'encourage risk taking' and lead to a more festive, lively and creative atmosphere conducive to interest, enjoyment and achievement.

4 Multiple intelligence theory encourages self-reflection among teachers:

- *Self-validation*: Teachers learnt to accept their own intelligences, which, in turn, boosted their self-confidence as teachers.
- *Colleague appreciation*: Acceptance of personal strengths and weaknesses led to greater appreciation of other teachers' styles.
- *Risk taking*: Teachers who understood the theory of multiple intelligences developed the courage to experiment: 'I previously thought that there were certain things I simply wasn't good at.'

If the findings of this survey are to be seen as generalisable, then there is certainly merit in adopting at least some of the approaches suggested by the theory of multiple intelligences. Awareness of one's particular intelligence strengths and weaknesses is a metacognitive understanding that can contribute to a learner's ability to operate at a metacognitive level when faced with particular learning situations or when faced with problems to solve.

Gardner is criticised (by, amongst others, Demetriou; see Demetriou *et al.* 1992) for underestimating the effects on his various intelligences by processes that define more general mental acuity. Examples of this more general acuity include speed of processing, executive functions (such as problem solving and verbal reasoning abilities), working memory, metacognitive awareness, underlying self-awareness and self-regulation. All of the above are integral and essential components of general intelligence, and, as such, they contribute to the regulation of the functioning and development of different domains of intelligence. That is, they are extremely likely to have effects on the perceived levels of Gardner's intelligences.

Summary

- Traditional measures of intelligence stress traditionally accepted definitions of intelligence, which are based extensively on a narrow range of skills, such as reading, writing and facility with numbers.

- There are other strengths demonstrated by many individuals who are clearly 'intelligent', but not skilled with words or numbers.

- It is possible to allow children to work to their strengths at the same time as fulfilling the requirements of a set curriculum.

We will consider aspects of Gardner's thoughts on multiple intelligences in the next chapter, since an individual's strengths and preferences for learning can be affected by particular strengths or weaknesses in any of Gardner's intelligences.

The Internet is a source of multiple intelligences testing and investigation. There are many sites where it is possible to undertake a short, questionnaire-style test that will lead to the production of an individual multiple intelligence profile. Naturally, the reliability of these sites must be considered, since some clearly take into account a great deal more than others when seeking out the individual's profile. A Google search using the phrase 'test your multiple intelligences' returns many hits. Refining this search will allow tests or inventories to be accessed. Caution is advised when using these sites.

In the classroom

- Be aware that individuals have different strengths and are likely to perform very differently according to the nature of the style of the tasks with which they are presented.

- Give opportunities for learning in a range of different ways; sitting and listening may suit some children, but others will find this particularly difficult; conversely, others will not respond well to individual work. Be flexible in teaching approaches.

- Give opportunities for learners to respond in a range of different ways; writing prose responses is not the only way to record events – indeed, there are many ways other than writing in which new learning can be dealt with.

- Be prepared to reward responses to work that do not necessarily conform to the traditional expectation of 'schoolwork'.

5

Learning styles

It is apparent to many of those who have considered learning, even if only in passing, that we learn in different ways from one another and we often choose to use what has become known as a 'preferred learning style'. The literature on the subject is vast and a full review of what has been written would take in many other related areas that deal with the same, or at least very similar and very closely related, ideas. Cognitive style, for example, is an area of psychology that investigates the preferred style of thinking and problem solving an individual may have. The term 'learning preferences' is also widely used to refer to what we shall here refer to as 'learning style'.

Over the last four decades or so – specifically, since the 1970s – there has been interest in the different ways in which we learn: learning style. This interest has been seen in the related fields of education, learning and psychology. Early work in this area is attributed to Kolb and Fry, who developed a theory of experiential learning (1974) that was instrumental in the development of Kolb's later work, and, indeed, the work of Honey and Mumford (see below) and others. However, as we tend to find in most areas of research, the tide sometimes reverses and ideas change or go out of fashion. As we will see, we seem to be at a time in the development of thinking in this area when there are challenges to what has become accepted, and applied, across many areas of the developed world.

The literature provides useful definitions of learning styles and related ideas that we could consider. To look briefly at one or two will act as a useful starting point.

Learning style is defined variously as:

- a particular way in which an individual learns;
- a mode of learning – an individual's preferred or best manner(s) in which to think, process information and demonstrate learning;
- an individual's preferred means of acquiring knowledge and skills;
- habits, strategies or regular mental behaviours concerning learning, particularly deliberate educational learning, that an individual displays.

Cognitive style is also defined in a range of different ways, such as:

- a certain approach to problem solving, based on intellectual schemes of thought;
- individual characteristics of cognitive processing that are peculiar to a particular individual;
- a person's typical approach to learning activities and problem solving;
- strategies, or regular mental behaviours, habitually applied by an individual to problem solving.

As we can see, there are many overlapping features contained within these definitions.

So, a learning style is a preferred way of learning and studying; for example, using pictures instead of text; working in groups as opposed to working alone; or learning in a structured rather than an unstructured manner. Learning preferences refer to an individual's preferred intellectual approach to learning, which has an important bearing on how learning proceeds for each individual, especially when considered in conjunction with what teachers expect from learners in the classroom. This idea will be explored later.

The term 'learning preferences' has been used to refer to the conditions – encompassing environmental, emotional, sociological and physical conditions – that an individual learner would choose, if they were in a position to make a choice (Dunn *et al.* 1989). Choice is another slant on the notion of preferred learning styles that has a bearing on how learning progresses. This is, perhaps, more to do with the general area of cognitive preferences, but is still important in this context.

If a particular approach to learning is encouraged by a teacher, there is a possibility that some pupils will work and learn less effectively than others in the class. For this reason, an awareness of learning styles is important for teachers. Learning style awareness should make an impact on pedagogy – the ways in which teachers choose to teach – and should help teachers to a better understanding of the needs of learners, as well as to an awareness of the need to differentiate materials, not only by level of difficulty but also by learning, and teaching, style.

The literature dealing with learning styles has something else to say that should be of interest to teachers. It is suggested that learners who are actively engaged in the learning process will be more likely to achieve success (Dewar 1996; Hartman 1995; Leadership Project 1995). Once learners become actively engaged in their own learning process, they develop a sense of being in control. This has been shown to improve self-esteem and motivation. A learner's awareness of learning preference and an understanding of the learning process, as well as metacognitive engagement, can lead to improved learning outcomes.

Learning styles

What becomes very clear, as we think closely about different learners who are known to us, is that they do not all learn in the same way. Each individual will adopt an approach to learning with which they are most comfortable, and, in doing so, leave behind the approaches with which they are less comfortable. It is helpful for learners if they are aware of their own particular learning preferences, as it will allow them to use an appropriate learning style to suit the particular learning that is being undertaken and to take opportunities to improve their potential for learning when faced with a learning activity that might steer them towards one of their 'weaker' – or, at least, one of their less favoured – styles.

The Honey–Mumford model

Learning styles are not fixed traits that an individual will always display. Learners are able to adopt different styles in different contexts. For most of us, one or two styles are preferred above the others. Honey and Mumford (1986) suggest that we need to be able to adopt one of four different styles in order to complete any given learning task satisfactorily. An inability or reluctance to adopt any particular style has the potential to hamper our ability to learn effectively.

The four styles described in the Honey-Mumford model are:

1 activist;
2 reflector;
3 theorist;
4 pragmatist.

Activists

Activists prefer to learn by doing rather than, for example, by reading or listening. They thrive on novelty and will 'give anything a try'. They like to immerse themselves in a wide range of experiences and activities, and like to work in groups so that ideas can be shared and ideas tested. They like to get on with things, meaning that they are not interested in planning. Activists are bored by repetition, and are most often open minded and enthusiastic.

Reflectors

Reflectors stand back and observe. They like to collect as much information as possible before making any decisions; they are always keen to 'look before they leap'. They prefer to look at the big picture, including previous experiences and the perspectives of others. The strength of reflectors is their painstaking data collection and its subsequent analysis, which will take place before any conclusion is reached. Reflectors are slow to make up their minds, but, when they do, their decisions are based on sound consideration of both their own knowledge and opinions and what they have taken in when watching and listening to the thoughts and ideas of others.

Theorists

Theorists like to adapt and integrate all of their observations into frameworks, so that they are able to see how one observation is related to other observations. Theorists work towards adding new learning into existing frameworks by questioning and assessing the possible ways that new information might fit into their existing frameworks of understanding. They have tidy and well-organised minds. They sometimes cannot relax until they get to the bottom of the situation in question and are able to explain their observations in basic terms. Theorists are uncomfortable with anything subjective or ambiguous. Theorists are usually sound in their approach to problem solving, taking a logical, one-step-at-a-time approach.

Pragmatists

Pragmatists are keen to seek out and make use of new ideas. Pragmatists look for the practical implications of any new ideas or theories before making a judgement on their value. They will take the view that, if something works, all is well and good, but, if it does not work, there is little point in spending time on the analysis of its failure. A strength of pragmatists is that they are confident in their use of new ideas and will incorporate them into their thinking. Pragmatists are most at home in problem-solving situations.

These four dimensions can be used as a way of classifying learners. The four basic types of learner, as characterised by preference for active, reflective, theoretical or practical learning, are clearly different, one from the other, but most learners are not extreme examples of just one preference. Most people have characteristics of all four dimensions. Honey and Mumford devised a learning style inventory, designed to help individuals to find out which predominant type of learner they might be.

Completing the inventory involves answering 'yes' or 'no' to 80 statements, 20 of which are related to each of the four types. The scores are then added up, plotted along the axes of a chart, and joined up to produce a kite shape of the type shown in Figure 5.1. The pattern in this diagram shows a typical pattern for a mature learner who can adopt any of the four learning styles when appropriate.

Neuro-linguistic programming

The next description of learning styles comes from a different, but obviously related, area of human research; namely, neuro-linguistic programming (NLP). Neuro-linguistic programming is concerned with how we communicate and how this affects our learning. Over many years, and through many research projects, including close and detailed observation of the way we communicate, three particular learning styles – visual, auditory and kinaesthetic (V–A–K) – have been identified.

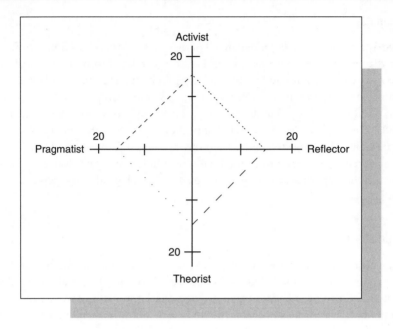

Figure 5.1 A sample Honey and Mumford 'kite'

Visual learners

Visual learners prefer to learn by seeing. They have good visual recall and prefer information to be presented visually; in the form of diagrams, graphs, maps, posters and displays, for example. They often use hand movements when describing or recalling events or objects and have a tendency to look upwards when thinking or recalling information.

Auditory learners

Auditory learners prefer to learn by listening. They have good auditory memory and benefit from discussion, lectures, interviewing, hearing stories and audio tapes, for example. They like sequence, repetition and summary, and, when recalling memories, tend to tilt their head and use level eye movements.

Kinaesthetic learners

Kinaesthetic learners prefer to learn by doing. They are good at recalling events and associate feelings or physical experiences with memory. They enjoy physical activity, field trips, manipulating objects and other practical, first-hand experience. They often find it difficult to keep still and need regular breaks in classroom activities.

While we all use all three styles of learning to some extent, some learners rely heavily on one of them. An overreliance on one style, and an inability or unwillingness to adopt another style where it might be appropriate, can be limiting in some learning situations and can mean that learning might be hindered.

An extension of the NLP description of learning styles has been developed by Fleming (2001). Fleming tells us that, when we gather information from the world around us, which includes the information that we need for learning, we make use of all of our senses. Some of us, though, employ one sense more than others. The V–A–R–K system assesses how much people rely on learning styles that are:

- visual;
- auditory;
- reading;
- kinaesthetic.

The Myers–Briggs model

The Myers-Briggs Type Indicator (MBTI) system is a means of establishing an individual's personality profile and is used widely in aptitude testing for employment. Designed as a tool for investigating the many different strands of personality type, the MBTI also has something for teachers to be aware of. The MBTI describes four personality types that can be interpreted along the lines of some of the other learning style descriptions.

The Myers-Briggs model (Briggs and Briggs Myers 1975; or Briggs and Myers 1980, for example) classifies individuals according to their preferences on scales derived from the theories of psychological types developed by Carl Jung. According to the model, learners may be:

- *extroverts* – who are happy to try things out and who focus on the world of people;
- *introverts* – who are more likely to think things through and to focus on the world of ideas;
- *sensors* – who tend to be practical, detail oriented and who focus on facts and procedures;
- *intuitors* – who are imaginative, concept oriented and focus on meaning;
- *thinkers* – who are sceptical and make decisions based on logic and rules;
- *feelers* – who are appreciative and tend to make decisions based on personal and more humanistic considerations;
- *judgers* – who set and follow agendas, and seek closure and completeness even without having the full picture; or
- *perceivers* – who adapt to changing circumstances and will defer completion until more is known.

The MBTI type preferences can be combined to give 16 different learning style types. For example, one learner may be an E–S–T–P (extrovert, sensor, thinker, perceiver) and another may be an I–N–F–J (introvert, intuitor, feeler, judger). Across all 16 types, there is a wide range of different types of learner, all of which can be found, in different proportions, in our classrooms. One element of the Myers-Briggs work that has become more commonly used is the introvert–extrovert continuum. This is perhaps a result of the Myers-Briggs types being based on Jung's work. Jung's main focus and subsequent work on personality types was on the introvert–extrovert dimension. The notion of an introvert or an extrovert has become widely understood outside the world of education or spheres of psychological study. The other dimensions have not.

According to the descriptions set out by the Myers-Briggs work, the following attributes and strengths relate to each of the different types defined.

Extrovert learners

Extrovert learners like to:

- talk to understand new information and ideas;
- work in groups;
- try something first and think about it later;
- see the results from a project;
- see examples of how other people are doing the work.

Strengths

Extroverts learn best when they can work with a friend and learn by trying something themselves instead of watching or listening to others. When they have difficulty with understanding, they benefit by talking about their ideas with others.

Introvert learners

Introvert learners like to:

- study alone;
- listen to others talk and think about information privately;
- think about something first and try it later;
- listen, observe, write and read;
- take time to complete assignments.

Strengths

Introverts learn best when they can find quiet places to work and have enough time to reflect on, redraft and improve their work. Introverts often like to make connections between schoolwork and their personal interests.

Sensing learners

Sensing learners:

- like clear goals;
- are careful and pay attention to details;
- like taking one step at a time;
- have a good memory for facts;
- pay more attention to practical tasks and ideas.

Strengths

Sensing learners learn best when they can ask their teacher to explain exactly what is expected and when they can focus on skills and tasks that are important in their lives. They like to use computers, watch films or find other ways to see, hear and touch what they are learning.

Intuitive learners

Intuitive learners:

- like reading and listening;
- like problems that require the use of imagination;
- like variety;
- are more interested in big ideas than in little details;
- like starting on new projects rather than finishing existing ones.

Strengths

Intuitive learners learn best when they can find ways to be imaginative and creative in school. They prefer to follow their instincts and understand the big picture before they begin school tasks.

Thinking learners

Thinking learners:

- want to be treated fairly;
- like teachers who are organised;
- want to feel a sense of achievement and skill;
- use clear thinking to work out problems;
- like clear and logical direction.

Strengths

Thinking learners learn best when they have limited time to do their work and are able to put information in a logical order that makes sense to them. They succeed when they can focus on what they already know in order to make connections to new information.

Feeling learners

Feeling learners:

- like to have a friendly relationship with teachers;
- learn by helping others;
- need to get along with other people;
- like to work with groups;
- like tasks with which they have a personal connection.

Strengths
Feeling learners learn best when they can work with a friend, find opportunities to choose topics they care about and help others.

Judging learners

Judging learners:

- like to have a plan and stick to it;
- work in a steady, orderly way;
- like to finish projects;
- take school seriously;
- like to know exactly what is expected of them.

Strengths
Judging learners learn best when they have short-term goals, when they are able to make a plan of action and find out from the teacher exactly what is expected.

Perceiving learners

Perceiving learners:

- are open to new experiences in learning;
- like to make choices;
- are flexible;
- work best when work is fun;
- like to discover new information.

Strengths
Perceiving learners learn best when they find new ways to do routine tasks in order to generate interest and to discover new information and ideas. They prefer

being involved in projects that are open ended without definite cut-off points and deadlines.

Studies show that many teachers are of the intuitive type, preferring abstract and theoretical ideas. This learning style preference is often reflected in how they plan for learning in their classrooms. The needs of their pupils, who will have a range of different learning types, are often neglected. We will return to this notion later.

The Kolb model

Yet another description of learning style is found in Kolb's 1984 *Learning Style* model, which classifies individuals over two continuous dimensions as having a preference for:

1 The *concrete experience* mode or the *abstract conceptualisation* mode (the dimension concerning how the learner takes in information).

2 The *active experimentation* mode or the *reflective observation* mode (the dimension concerning how the learner internalises information).

Kolb (1984) describes four general learning types based on the two dimensions, as follows:

1 *Type 1: Diverger (concrete, reflective).* Type 1 learners often use the question 'Why?' and they respond well to explanations of how new material relates to their experience and interests. Diverging learners prefer to learn by observation, brainstorming and gathering information. They are imaginative and sensitive.

2 *Type 2: Assimilator (abstract, reflective).* Type 2 learners often use the question 'What?' and respond well to information presented in an organised, logical fashion. They benefit if they are given time for reflection. Assimilating learners prefer to learn by putting information in concise logical order and using reflective observation.

3 *Type 3: Converger (abstract, active).* Type 3 learners often use the question 'How?' and respond to having opportunities to work actively on well-defined tasks. They learn by trial and error in an environment that allows them to fail safely. Converging learners like to learn by solving problems and doing technical tasks, and are good at finding practical uses for ideas.

4 *Type 4: Accommodator (concrete, active).* Type 4 learners often use the question 'What if?' and respond well when they are able to apply new material in problem-solving situations. Accommodating learners are people-oriented, hands-on learners and rely on feelings rather than logic.

Figure 5.2 gives a pictorial explanation of the way that the dimensions interact to give the four learning types. Kolb says that, while almost every individual makes use of all learning modes to some extent, each person has a preferred learning style.

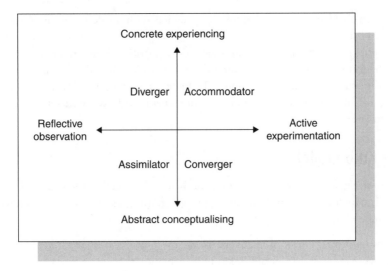

Figure 5.2 Kolb's dimensions

The Felder–Silverman model

The Felder–Silverman learning style model (1988) is another system for describing learning style. It has many similarities with the other systems, and classifies learners as:

- *sensing learners* – who prefer the concrete, are practical and are oriented toward facts and procedures; or *intuitive learners* – who prefer the conceptual, are innovative, and oriented towards theories and meanings;

- *visual learners* – who prefer visual representations of material (pictures, diagrams, flow charts); or *verbal learners* – who prefer written and spoken explanations;

- *inductive learners* – who prefer to consider topics by moving from the specific to the general; or *deductive learners* – who prefer to consider topics by moving from the general to the specific;

- *active learners* – who learn by trying things out and working with others; or *reflective learners* – who learn by thinking things through and working alone;

- *sequential learners* – who prefer to work in a linear, orderly fashion and prefer to learn in small incremental steps; or *global learners* – who prefer to take a holistic view and learn by taking large steps forward.

Learning styles and multiple intelligences

Gardner and Hatch conclude that it may be worthwhile for teachers to 'detect the distinctive human strengths and use them as a basis for engagement and learning' (1990). They describe this process, unsurprisingly, in terms of multiple intelligences, which we have considered in the previous chapter, and, in doing so, demonstrate the many overlaps between multiple intelligence theory and the area of study on which this chapter focuses; namely, learning styles.

If we look, in Table 5.1, at each of the intelligences in turn and consider the way in which those learners with particular strengths in the area in question might best learn, we can devise a set of ideas that could be of practical use in the planning of learning activities.

TABLE 5.1 Learning activity preferences for the different intelligences

Intelligence	Preferences
Linguistic/verbal learner: intelligence related to language and to the written and spoken word	■ Likes to: read, write and tell stories, work with riddles. ■ Is good at: using descriptive language, memorising places, dates and trivia. ■ Learns best by: saying, hearing and seeing words.
Logical/mathematical learner: intelligence related to reasoning, numbers, abstractions and patterns	■ Likes to: do experiments, work things out, work with numbers, ask questions and explore patterns and relationships. ■ Is good at: maths, reasoning, logic and problem solving, working from concrete to abstract. ■ Learns best by: categorising, classifying and working with abstract patterns and relationships.
Spatial/visual learner: intelligence related to anything visual and the creation of mental images	■ Likes to: draw, build, design and create things, daydream, look at pictures and slides, watch films and play with machines. ■ Is good at: imagining things, sensing changes, mazes and puzzles, and reading maps and charts. ■ Learns best by: visualising, dreaming, using the 'mind's eye' and working with pictures.
Kinaesthetic learner: intelligence related to physical movement and actions located in the brain's motor cortex (where movement is controlled)	■ Likes to: move around, touch, 'tinker', talk, use body language and perform. ■ Is good at: physical activities and crafts. ■ Learns best by: touching, moving, interacting with space and processing knowledge through bodily sensations.
Musical learner: intelligence related to sounds and auditory patterns, to rhythm, beat and tempo	■ Likes to: play musical instruments, sing, drum. Likes the sound of the human voice. ■ Is good at: listening, inventing tunes, keeping time (tempo), discriminating between different sounds. ■ Learns best by: listening, especially if things are set to music or are rhythmical.

(Continued)

TABLE 5.1 Continued

Intelligence	Preferences
Interpersonal learner: intelligence related to relationships with others and various means of communication	■ Likes to: have lots of friends, talk to people, solve problems and join groups. ■ Is good at: understanding other people's feelings, leading others, organising and communicating. ■ Learns best by: sharing, comparing, relating and talking.
Intrapersonal learner: intelligence related to self-reflection and self-awareness	■ Likes to: work alone and pursue own interests, daydream. ■ Is good at: understanding self, focusing inwards on feelings and dreams, following instincts, pursuing interests/goals and being original. ■ Learns best by: working alone, individualised projects, self-paced instruction and having own space.
Naturalistic learner: intelligence related to observation and awareness of the natural world and the patterns to be found there	■ Likes to: work outdoors, or at least close to the natural environment. ■ Is good at: collecting and classifying, identifying natural artefacts. ■ Learns best by: working outdoors, relating classroom ideas and activities to the natural world.

There was a great deal of research carried out in the later part of the twentieth century (Della Valle *et al.* 1986; Dunn *et al.* 1982; Lemmon 1985; MacMurren 1985) concerned with identifying the relationship between academic achievement and individual learning style. The research has produced fairly consistent support for the following ideas:

■ Pupils do learn in different ways to one another.

■ Pupil performance in different subject areas is related to how individuals learn.

■ When pupils are taught with approaches and resources that complement their particular learning styles, their achievement is significantly increased.

The third of these points has importance for teachers if they are to develop approaches to teaching all pupils that will ensure that the greatest number of learners in their classes benefit from their teaching. Another interesting but, in the light of what has gone before, possibly quite obvious pointer from the research is that children are far more likely to complete their homework if 'its design takes into consideration students' learning styles and study habits' (Dunn *et al.* 1989).

By learning about the learning style preferences of learners, teachers put themselves in a far stronger position when they come to the task of planning learning approaches and classroom activities that are most likely to take advantage of pupils' individual learning styles, which will, in turn, help them to achieve their learning goals.

Problems can arise for teachers who try to explain things in a way that they consider everyone can understand when some of their pupils have difficulty in making sense of what they are being taught. From what we have seen, a pupil of a different temperament, whose mind is set in a different way from his or her teacher's – in short, with a different learning style – is likely to have the greatest difficulty.

It is highly likely to be of great value if both teachers and pupils can have awareness of the potential problems that differences in learning style and preference may lead to. That is, they should (in particular, the teacher should) be fully aware that we all learn in different ways, behave in different ways and go about our lives in different ways. We do not have to lose consideration for other people by encouraging differences. Parents, too, can benefit from knowledge of these differences, as it can impact on the approaches they might take when supporting their children's schoolwork at home.

From the point of view of the teacher, then, the important point about learning styles is not to be concerned with how many styles are listed, nor how they might be labelled, but to raise awareness in both teacher and learner that everyone is likely to learn in a different way, and that different learning styles present needs that must be met if teaching is to be effective and learning is to take place.

According to Bandler and Grinder (1979), 70 per cent of learners will be able to cope however a lesson is presented; 10 per cent will be unable to learn whichever method is employed, for reasons largely unrelated to learning style; but the remainder will only be able to learn in a visual, auditory or kinaesthetic way. It should, perhaps, be the view of teachers that 70 per cent is not enough and that some action needs to be taken in order to increase this figure. So, what should we do about this?

One view on the question of what to do with what we have learnt about individual learning styles is summed up by a set of notes lodged on the psychology department's website at the University of Glasgow:

> Should teachers adapt to learners, or learners to teachers? The answer is 'both'; and the concept to think of is that of learning communities. All (institutional) learning can be thought of from a wholly social perspective, as one of the learner joining a community, and becoming enculturated. From that point of view, the learner needs to do the adapting, and, the more they do so, the more they gain access to that subculture and its knowledge.
>
> The complementary viewpoint is that teachers should adapt, not so much to individuals as to the broadest audience possible, to make their material accessible to the most people.
>
> (Draper 2012)

From this perspective, the onus is on both teacher and learner. However, since it is the prime role of a teacher to facilitate and encourage learning in all of their pupils, it is fairly clear that the real responsibility to accommodate lies with the teacher. Naturally, though, some accommodating is also required on the part of the learner.

What is perhaps needed is an approach that is sometimes referred to as 'teaching to all types'. This is not always as straightforward as some would have us believe, of course. An example of how to teach to all types, which can also be described as 'appealing to a wide range of learning styles', based on, for example, the Felder–Silverman model, might look something like this:

- For the *sensing/intuitive* continuum: balance concrete information, such as facts and experimental results, with conceptual information, such as theories and models and ideas.

- For the *visual/verbal* continuum: make use of graphs, diagrams, pictures and demonstrations as well as spoken and written explanations of the same information; learners can make a choice of which resources to use.

- For the *inductive/deductive* continuum: ask pupils to reason and attempt to explain a general principle given only experimental observations to work with, as well as exploring principles based on their component parts.

- For the *active/reflective* continuum: provide time for pupils to consider the material presented, possibly individually, as well as time for active participation in group work.

- For the *sequential/global* learner: be sure to highlight the logical flow of material, but also make connections to other lessons, topics and everyday experiences. Encourage both logical, linear thought patterns and the wider, sometimes referred to as 'lateral', patterns of thought.

There are other, similar sets of instructions that have been prepared for teachers to consider when making plans for learning. The lists refer to learning preferences and suggest particular activities that are likely to satisfy all of, or at least as many of the different preferences that are likely to be encountered. Indeed, Table 5.1 sets out the particular approaches that are likely to be favoured by, and therefore successful with, learners having different preferences and strengths.

We should perhaps bear in mind, however, that the educational system in most countries, and particularly in the developed world, rewards and even requires learning and, in particular, successful learning outcomes, in terms of examination passes, to be approached through language – more specifically, written language. This has ramifications for what goes on in classrooms. While teachers have a view to providing appropriate learning activities for a range of different learning styles, they must also have a clear grip on the fact that success in our current educational climate depends heavily upon reading and writing.

Identifying learning styles

We have seen that it is helpful for teachers to consider the learning styles of their pupils and for them to incorporate what they discover into their approach to planning – at an individual level sometimes. There are formal tests and quizzes designed to identify learning styles, and some schools make use of them. There are some examples available online and a simple search will unearth them. Naturally, each learning style 'quiz' or inventory will be designed to categorise learners according to the theoretical position on learning styles taken by its creators. It is possible to find formal ways of identifying learning styles to suit the preferred descriptions of learning styles available, some of which we have considered earlier. There are also similar tests or quizzes available to help in the identification of multiple intelligence strengths and preferences. Some schools or individual teachers like to encourage their pupils to consider their particular learning styles, and some of the online quizzes are helpful at this level.

In some cases, teachers do not want to go as far as formally examining the learning styles of a class, but would still like insight into an individual's style in order to be able to understand better how they are likely to function in learning situations. It appears that, at a simple level, it is possible to pick up on some visual cues that give an idea of an individual's style. Put simply, and as we saw earlier, visual learners tend to look up (for a mental picture, perhaps), auditory learners tend to look to the side and kinaesthetic learners tend to look down. The reasons for this are not given in any of the easily available sources, but it does seem, as a rule of thumb, to be useful.

There is a possible drawback to helping children to identify their particular learning style: if a child is given a particular learning style label, it is possible that they will centre their learning on this one approach to learning and even refuse to work in other modes. This would be undesirable. When introducing the idea of learning styles to children, it is probably helpful to stress the importance of being able to work and learn in different ways at different times and for different purposes. A case – even a strong case – for encouraging children to develop ways of learning that do not come easily to them can be made.

Research exploring learning styles

Dunn and Dunn (1978) have undertaken research within the sphere of the V–A–K classification. They point out that learning styles will differ widely amongst learners in the classroom, and that teachers should attempt to make changes in their teaching approaches that will be of benefit to learners of every learning style. Included in their suggestions for changes are: room layout and design, the development of small-group work and the development of what they call 'contract activity packages'. This refers to the planning of activities, including:

- a clear statement of the learning need;
- multisensory resources (relating to auditory, visual, and kinaesthetic styles);
- activities through which the newly mastered information can be used creatively;
- the sharing of creative projects within small groups;
- at least three small-group techniques;
- a pre-test, a self-test and a post-test.

Redesigning the classroom involves such things as fitting movable partitions that can be used to arrange the room in a range of different ways, in order to allow for what Dunn and Dunn call different learning stations and instructional areas.

A report on the scientific validity of learning styles and practices based on the theory of learning styles (Pashler *et al.* 2009) cast doubt on the usefulness to teachers, and others, of considering different learning styles in their practice. The panel who prepared the report came to the view that no adequate evaluation of the learning styles had been undertaken, and, for that reason, the real value of what is referred to as the 'learning style hypothesis' (which states that, for optimal learning to take place, learners should be taught in a manner that is strictly tailored to their learning styles) remains unproven. The report says that, in order to fully and rigorously test the hypothesis, learners should be grouped into the learning style categories that are being evaluated (e.g. auditory learners compared with verbal learners), and then learners in each group must be assigned randomly to a particular learning method (e.g. auditory learning or verbal learning); in this way, some learners will be matched with their particular style and others mismatched. At the end of the experiment, all learners should take an identical assessment. If the learning style hypothesis is to be shown as valid, auditory learners should learn better with auditory teaching methods and visual learners should learn better with visual methods, for example. Other writers in the field (e.g. Massa and Mayer 2006) have come to the same conclusion. They make the claim that the usefulness of paying great attention to learning styles and matching them with teaching approaches is not proven.

Pashler *et al.* reported that studies using their approved research design were virtually absent from the learning styles literature, and they were only able to find a small number of studies with which they were satisfied in this respect (2009). Of the studies that did meet their criteria, only one had positive findings to report. Mostly, they found that the same learning approach produced similar outcomes for learners across the spectrum of learning styles (Massa and Mayer 2006).

The report also pointed out that the benefits of tailoring teaching closely to learning style needs would need to be very great before learning style interventions could be recommended as a cost-effective way forward. As it was, in their view, any benefits shown, even if they were statistically significant, were simply not enough to justify the use of learning style-based approaches over other potential approaches for specific cases, such as one-to-one support or other interventions that are often in place.

Pashler's panel (2009) concluded that: '[A]t present, there is no adequate evidence base to justify incorporating learning styles assessments into general educational practice. Thus, limited education resources would better be devoted to adopting other educational practices that have strong evidence base, of which there are an increasing number.'

Research with the aim of evaluating teaching styles and learning styles (Spoon and Schell 1998) has found that congruent groups have no significant differences in achievement from incongruent groups. They also found that style in this study varied by age, which suggests that changes in learning style may take place as we get older and, by default, become more experienced. The findings of this study call into question the strong claims made for matching teaching to pupil learning.

Some psychologists and neuroscientists have questioned the scientific and research basis for models of learning styles and the theories on which they are based. For example, Susan Greenfield, writing in the *Times Educational Supplement* (2007), said that: 'From a neuroscientific point of view, [the learning styles approach to teaching] is nonsense.' Stahl (2002) considers there to have been what he describes as an 'utter failure to find that assessing children's learning styles and matching to instructional methods has any effect on their learning'. Also, Coffield *et al.* (2004a; 2004b) found that none of the learning style theories currently considered to be valid had been adequately studied and vindicated by independent researchers, leading them to conclude, for example, that the notions of visual, auditory and kinaesthetic preferences, as well as the value of attempting to match teaching and learning styles, were all 'highly questionable'.

A criticism often levelled at the learning styles lobby is that the evidence gathered relies, in a large part, on the analysis of self-assessment questionnaires, with children being asked to confirm, often by simply ticking boxes, the activities they like and the ways of thinking and working that they find easy or difficult. Sceptics question whether primary school children, in particular, have the ability to analyse the way, or ways, in which they work. There is also the fact that many school activities are not purely visual, auditory or kinaesthetic, but quite often a blend of all three. A child may be looking at a book (visual) while listening to a teacher (auditory) and making notes (kinaesthetic); many practical activities depend upon listening and, perhaps, reading if they are to be accomplished successfully. There are also questions raised concerning the labels themselves and the links between particular learning styles and specific subjects. If a child likes drama, does that make them a kinaesthetic learner, or does it perhaps mean that they are keen on performing and good at taking on roles?

As reported in the *Times Educational Supplement* (Hastings 2012), Bricheno has looked at the impact of a learning styles approach on pupil attitudes. Initially, her interviews suggested that all children had a leaning towards kinaesthetic style learning activities. On closer examination of her data, however, it seemed not to be so clear cut. By delving deeper into the scenarios that she had investigated, what she discovered was that many of the kinaesthetic activities referred to were undertaken in groups, and that what the pupils questioned actually preferred was working with others, not the nature of the activity itself. Furthermore, Bricheno has previously acknowledged 'the difficulty of measuring and identifying students' preferred learning styles' (Bricheno and Younger 2004).

In a 'systematic and critical review of learning styles', Coffield *et al.* (2004a) acknowledge what they call the 'enormous intuitive appeal in the idea that teachers should pay closer attention to students' learning styles'. However, they also identify significant problems that affect the view taken of learning styles, which is often accepted and promulgated. Importantly, they say that they found very sparse evidence to suggest that teaching influenced by the idea of learning styles has a significant effect on achievement or motivation. Their review continues by stating that they found an emphasis away from learning and towards learner characteristics, which has the effect of reducing the importance of acquiring subject knowledge. They also say that the theoretical and practical applications of many of the leading models of learning style preference are under-researched.

In concluding, the review states that the implications for teaching and learning that arise from interest in learning styles models are not new and that much of the research which they reviewed did not go much further than suggesting that a variety of teaching approaches could benefit learners. The theorists do, however, have considerably different views in terms of what teachers should provide for a learner with a particular learning style. These views seem to stretch from one extreme to the other, and range from the need to match teaching and learning styles to the need to extend the repertoire of learning skills for individuals.

Summary

Individual learners have preferred ways of working, thinking and learning. If an individual's preferred approach to learning tasks is ignored in the ways that a teacher expects them to work, there is a distinct possibility that their learning will not progress as efficiently and effectively as it might.

Descriptions of learning styles are plentiful – and some are complex. One description commonly used to help teachers understand differences in a practical and immediate way is the 'visual–auditory–kinaesthetic' range of styles. It is likely that one-third of any given class will have a preference for learning that is undertaken in one of these divisions. This means that teachers should be aware of, and take into account, the fact that some of their pupils will find it difficult to make headway with their learning if at least some of it is not presented in an appropriate format for them.

It is very important that opportunities are given to learners of all types to take part fully in the planned learning activities in classrooms, and that they should have full access to the curriculum, whatever their learning style preference might be.

It should be remembered that, as with many concerns within the field of education and elsewhere, there are sometimes research findings that contradict what has become an accepted part of established practice. This is what makes many fields exciting and dynamic, and what leads to change and improvement. Some research has shown that the strength of the learning styles hypothesis is not as great as it has been believed to be, and this should be taken into account by academics and practitioners alike.

In the classroom

In some ways, the suggestions that might be added at the end of this chapter are very similar to those at the end of the previous chapter on multiple intelligences. We have discussed the links between multiple intelligences and learning styles, and it is reasonable to repeat the points from Chapter 4 here:

- Be aware that individuals have different strengths and are likely to perform very differently according to the nature of the style of the tasks with which they are presented.

- Give opportunities for learning in a range of different ways; sitting and listening may suit some children, but others will find this particularly difficult; conversely, others will not respond well to individual work. Be flexible in teaching approaches.

- Give opportunities for learners to respond in a range of different ways; writing prose responses is not the only way to record events; indeed, there are many ways other than writing that new learning can be dealt with.

- Be prepared to reward responses to work that do not necessarily conform to the traditional expectation of 'schoolwork'.

- Help learners to realise that there is more than one way to approach and solve a learning problem, and that one approach is almost certainly as valid as another if it leads to the required outcome.

6

Difficulties with learning

This chapter will provide an overview of some of the special needs that may be encountered in classrooms and will consider their underlying causes. There will also be a brief consideration of how best to deal with some of the manifestations of special needs in an attempt to maximise the learning of those children who are affected.

An important consideration for a book of this nature is the potential that learners have for difficulties or setbacks with their learning. What we might call 'normal' – that is, following a route through learning and intellectual development that might be wholly expected – does not apply to all learners. Indeed, the very notion of normal might be scoffed at since all learners have unique attributes, strengths and weaknesses – but it is possible to pencil in a simple divide between relatively straightforward learning progression and learning that is problematic and dogged by difficulty of one sort or another. In reality, a dividing line is not a useful tool since the range of learning ability is probably best represented by a continuum from 'extremely difficult' to 'non-problematic'. However, even this description is not ideal. For most learners, there are certain areas of learning that present problems. A clear example of this might be the case of dyslexia. Some children diagnosed with dyslexia, the definitions of which we will consider later, have extreme difficulty with reading, spelling and the like, but excel in other areas of the curriculum. Another group of learners who have widespread and general learning difficulties often find learning, of any sort, in any area of experience, incredibly difficult. It is possible for all of us, no matter what our station in life, no matter what educational success we may have achieved, to identify certain areas of learning that we consider particularly difficult or troublesome. This is quite likely to be a function of much of what has gone before in this book – styles, preferences, differing balance of intelligences and so on. For others, as we will see, there are particular barriers to learning that lead to a range of problems, including poor performance, lowered self-esteem and even bad behaviour.

If we look, first, at some of the more theoretical generalities of learning difficulties, it will allow us to understand better the manifestations in classrooms, in terms of pupil behaviour and attitude, of the outward signs of some of the more common difficulties, their particular problems and some strategies for dealing with them.

General learning difficulties – higher-level descriptions

The model of learning disabilities that is currently most widely used evolved during the 1960s. Four stages of information processing used in learning are identified and difficulties experienced by learners are categorised accordingly. The four stages are:

1 *Input*: the process of taking in and recording information that has been received via the senses.
2 *Integration*: the process whereby information is interpreted, categorised, placed in sequence and linked with previous learning.
3 *Memory*: the stage where information is placed into storage for later retrieval and use.
4 *Output*: the time when actions are taken based on the processing of stored information; this can be in the form of language or of action (e.g. movements or gestures).

Learning disabilities are classified by their effects at one or more of these stages. Each child is likely to have individual strengths and weaknesses at each of the stages.

Difficulties with input

All of our senses contribute towards the total input that we receive. In terms of classroom learning, the most used senses are vision and hearing, although the others naturally have a role to play too. Problems with visual perception can mean that the shape, size, position, orientation and even colour of objects, including, most crucially, letters, can be distorted or even indistinguishable.

Problems with auditory perception can mean that the voice of the teacher is not heard accurately, parts of instructions not detected at all and the subtle discrimination of letter sounds may be lost or altered in some way.

Difficulties with integration

When information is processed, it is ordered and sequenced, interpreted and categorised. New items of information are classified and considered in relation to other, previously learnt information (see 'schemas', Chapter 3). Examples of processing difficulties are the inability to retell a story in the correct sequence, inability to memorise particular sequences, such as the months or seasons, and the inability to generalise a concept to other areas of understanding.

Difficulties with memory

Memory difficulties can be with either the short-term (working) memory or, less often, with the long-term memory. Difficulties with the visual memory, associated with remembering what has just been seen, can lead to problems with reading, writing and spelling. Most memory problems are associated with short-term memory, which means that many more repetitions of new material need to be made if learning is to develop (see 'over-teaching', below).

Difficulties with output

For humans, in this context, output refers to language – sounds – or to muscular activity – gestures, expressions, mark making (writing or drawing).

Difficulties with language usually refer to spoken language and the inability to function effectively by means of the spoken word. This can, for example, manifest itself when a child is required to answer a question and is unable to recall the necessary information in order to formulate a response. Difficulties can be characterised by the inability to marshal thoughts sufficiently well for them to be put into clear spoken words.

Difficulties with motor skills can be either fine or gross. Fine motor skill difficulties lead to trouble with, most notably in the classroom, handwriting, drawing and colouring, and such things as using scissors accurately. Gross motor skill problems lead to general clumsiness and difficulty with games that rely on good co-ordination. Running may be problematic for children with problems of this nature, as can learning to ride a bike.

Causes

The causes of difficulties of problems under the four stages listed above (input, integration, memory, output) are not always obvious, and, in some ways, from the point of view of managing classroom tasks and activities, not crucially relevant. However, a simple overview of some of the known causes of these difficulties is given below.

For the sake of simplicity, the possible causes are divided into two groups; first, those present at birth and of a genetic or physical problem during the birth (referred to as 'congenital', meaning a condition present at birth, whether inherited or caused by the birth environment) and, second, those caused by events or situations that occur at some point after birth.

Causes related to genetics or difficulties at birth include:

- smaller than usual brain (microcephaly);
- a chromosome abnormality; for example, Down's syndrome;
- an abnormal accumulation of fluid in parts of the brain (hydrocephalus), which causes enlargement of the skull and compression of the brain that can destroy neural tissue;

- complications at birth, such as starvation of oxygen;
- mother's age at conception.

There are many other congenital conditions that can adversely affect a child's all-round development and lead to difficulties with learning, but many of them are exceedingly rare. Some show obvious outward signs; others do not.

Causes related to post-birth, environmental effects include:

- malnutrition;
- infectious diseases, such as meningitis;
- head injuries;
- exposure to alcohol and drugs or other hazardous substances;
- physical or mental/emotional abuse.

In many ways, the precise root cause of a particular child's difficulties may not be crucially important to a classroom practitioner, and, in many cases, precise causes are hard to establish. What matters is the precise manifestation of the difficulties and an insight into how best to deal with the problems that present themselves. It is important to note here that the scope of this chapter will not allow detailed diagnostic and remedial advice to be presented, but the overview given here, and the links to more detailed sources, will prove useful. It is also important to bear in mind that the diagnoses of many of the more persistent problems that arise in learning are the domain of professionals with expertise either in the appropriate medical or psychological discipline, or in special educational needs. These professionals range from support teachers (usually, teachers with additional qualifications working from a central service such as a local authority learning support service) to specialist educational psychologists and others in the medical profession. For most immediate support with a child's learning problems, the school special educational needs co-ordinator would be the first point of contact.

General learning difficulties – educational and working definitions

When the difficulties that the causes described above can lead to are considered in more practical light – in government publications aimed at supporting teachers at work in classrooms, for example – there is, understandably, more emphasis given to the effects of the particular conditions on educational and intellectual development than on attempting to understand the detail of the underlying causes. The approaches to dealing with them are also considered in publications of this nature.

Although from 2000, the extract below, which is from a version of the code of practice for dealing with children's special educational needs in schools, gives a suitable and enduring definition of what we are considering here:

4.1 The nature and range of general learning difficulties. General learning difficulties may show themselves in the following ways:

- low levels of attainment across the board in all forms of assessment, including, for young children, baseline assessments;
- difficulty in acquiring skills (notably, in literacy and numeracy) on which much other learning in school depends;
- difficulty in dealing with abstract ideas and generalising from experience;
- a range of associated difficulties; notably, in speech and language (particularly for younger children) and in social and emotional development.

(DfEE 2000a)

Specific learning difficulties – commonly encountered problems

More space is devoted in this chapter to considering dyslexia than any of the other diagnosable problems that are dealt with. This is because it is now recognised as being far more complex and widespread a problem than originally thought, because all classrooms will have a percentage of pupils with dyslexia (up to one in ten, as we will see), and because, as a result of its history and its complexity, it is commonly misunderstood, or even disregarded as a myth by some (even by some in the teaching profession).

This is not the place to delve into the intricacies of teaching methods for dyslexic pupils, but, in considering the nature of dyslexia, we will look at the background and varying definitions, and, briefly, at the main approaches which are deemed to be effective when teaching children who are dyslexic.

Dyslexia is a specific learning disability that presents children and adults alike with problems, in a variety of combinations, concerning reading, writing, spelling, visual and auditory perception, organisational skills and memory. Often, this is coupled with difficulties with maths. It is widely accepted that dyslexia affects 10 per cent of the UK population and that 4 per cent are badly affected (Dyslexia Institute Limited 2008; DfEE 2000b). Those affected come

TABLE 6.1 Specific learning and motor skills disorders

Dyslexia	Any of various reading disorders associated with impairment of the ability to interpret spatial relationships or to integrate auditory and visual information.
Dyscalculia	A lack of the ability to solve mathematical problems, and difficulties with numbers generally.
Dyspraxia	An inability to perform coordinated movements; excessive clumsiness.

from all levels of society and from all different backgrounds. They also have the full range of intellectual and general abilities. It is known that it affects more boys than girls, and that there is an inherited factor. Recently, a gene has been identified that is believed to be responsible for transmitting the problems of dyslexia from parent to child.

Dyslexia

We are told, by the largest support association for dyslexia in the UK, that if we were to 'peruse ten different publications about dyslexia [we would] come across ten different definitions' (BDA 2008). By actually perusing a range of definitions, it becomes clear that, at a simple level, there is overlap and agreement, but, for some definitions, particularly the earlier ones, the question of general intelligence – at either a high, average or low level – seems to have particular significance. The question of general intelligence and problems of all-round learning difficulty are not considered wholly relevant, as we will see, in the most recent offerings, although cognitive abilities and the mismatch between reading ability and other abilities (the so-called 'discrepancy') do feature in one of them.

Below are some examples of definitions, beginning with one from 1968, when dyslexia was even less well understood than it is now, and finishing with the British Dyslexia Association's updated and most recent version.

World Federation of Neurology (1968): [Dyslexia is] a disorder in children who, despite conventional classroom experience, fail to attain the language skills of reading, writing and spelling commensurate with their intellectual abilities.

(Waites 1968)

Orton Dyslexia Society (1994): Dyslexia is one of several distinct learning disabilities. It is a specific language-based disorder of constitutional origin characterized by difficulties in single word decoding, usually reflecting insufficient phonological processing. These difficulties in single word decoding are often unexpected in relation to age and other cognitive and academic abilities; they are not the result of generalized developmental disability or sensory impairment. Dyslexia is manifest by variable difficulty with different forms of language, often including, in addition to problems with reading, a conspicuous problem with acquiring proficiency in writing and spelling.

(Reid-Lyon 1995)

British Dyslexia Association (1996): Dyslexia is a complex neurological condition that is constitutional in origin. The symptoms may affect many areas of learning and function, and may be described as a specific difficulty in reading, spelling and written language. One or more of these areas may be affected. Numeracy, notational skills (music), motor function and organizational skills may also be involved. However, it is particularly related to mastering written language, although oral language may be affected to some degree.

(Crisfield 1996)

British Psychological Society (1999): Dyslexia is evident when accurate and fluent word reading and/or spelling develops very incompletely or with great difficulty. This focuses on literacy learning at the 'word level' and implies that the problem is severe and persistent despite appropriate learning opportunities.

(BPS 1999)

British Dyslexia Association (2009): Dyslexia is a specific learning difficulty that mainly affects the development of literacy and language-related skills. It is likely to be present at birth and to be lifelong in its effects. It is characterised by difficulties with phonological processing, rapid naming, working memory, processing speed, and the automatic development of skills that may not match up to an individual's other cognitive abilities. It tends to be resistant to conventional teaching methods, but its effects can be mitigated by appropriately specific intervention, including the application of information technology and supportive counselling.

(BDA 2009)

Sir Jim Rose authored a report in 2009 titled 'Identifying and teaching children and young people with dyslexia and literacy difficulties' in which the following description of dyslexia was provided:

■ Dyslexia is a learning difficulty that primarily affects the skills involved in accurate and fluent word reading and spelling.

■ Characteristic features of dyslexia are difficulties in phonological awareness, verbal memory and verbal processing speed.

■ Dyslexia occurs across the range of intellectual abilities.

■ It is best thought of as a continuum, not a distinct category, and there are no clear cut-off points.

■ Co-occurring difficulties may be seen in aspects of language, motor co-ordination, mental calculation, concentration and personal organisation, but these are not, by themselves, markers of dyslexia.

■ A good indication of the severity and persistence of dyslexic difficulties can be gained by examining how the individual responds or has responded to well founded intervention.

Soon after the publication of the Rose report, this definition was adopted by the management board of the BDA. In adopting the definition, the BDA made the proviso that there should be an additional paragraph appended (BDA 2009), which is included here:

■ In addition to these characteristics, the BDA acknowledges the visual and auditory processing difficulties that some individuals with dyslexia can experience, and points out that dyslexic readers can show a combination of abilities and difficulties that affect the learning process. Some also have strengths in other areas, such as design, problem solving, creative skills, interactive skills and oral skills.

It seems possible that the definition of dyslexia arose as a means of explaining reading difficulty in children with high general intelligence, as opposed to children with low intelligence or more quantifiable brain disorders. Some writers (Stanovich 1996; Frith 1999) suggest that the intelligence-reading performance deficit (that is, children with average or above general intelligence but very poor reading development) is irrelevant, and that, in all probability, the underlying causes may be the same. The causes may be the same, but, anecdotally, some specialist teachers suggest that there is a clear difference in the way that these different groups of children respond to intensive specialist teaching. Those with average or above general intelligence make more progress in response to specific, tailored teaching programmes, and those with low general intelligence often do not. Memory seems to be a crucial factor here, and we are told that in many cases a child with dyslexia can remember something on a 'good day', but not at other times. If memory problems were not present, then it would be expected that children with average or above general intelligence would benefit from teaching, and remember the spelling rules, and the like, that they were taught.

For about 60 per cent of people with dyslexia, acquiring the skills required for basic maths is also difficult. Many people with dyslexia, however, have strong creative talents in the arts, design, computing and lateral thinking. During a child's early school years, dyslexia may affect self-esteem to such an extent that, until it is properly diagnosed and remedial teaching put in place, the child may refuse to read or write, appear 'stupid' to his peers, and generally find life very confusing and worrying. If support is not provided at an early stage, problems of low self-esteem continue and worsen, leading to additional stress and demotivation.

Identifying a child with dyslexia

Over the years, many individuals with undiagnosed dyslexia have been through the school system, done very badly in their work, and left school with no qualifications and a very poor self-image. (There are many counterexamples to this, of course.)

It is often difficult to detect the precise causes of child's difficulty with schoolwork and teachers have been known to put lack of progress down to many different causes, including laziness. When children are underachieving, especially in the sphere of reading and writing, a teacher should make certain investigations to establish if additional specialised help might be needed. This specialised help would be in the form of expert assessment and diagnosis, in the first instance.

In the case of poor progress, and more than expected difficulty with reading and writing, the following questions should be answered:

- Does the child have a history of delayed speech development, or generally poor articulation?
- Does the child have problems with visual perception? Do they frequently reverse letters and numbers?
- Does the child have problems with auditory perception? (This is more than a 'hearing' problem; it concerns difficulties in identifying separate sounds in words and being able to manipulate them.)
- Does the child have problems when integrating sensory information; for example, sounds and symbols, associating printed symbols (letters) with the correct sound?
- Does the child have poor or confused lateralisation (handedness), including underdeveloped hand–eye preferences and a confused sense of direction?
- Does the child have weak sequencing skills, sometimes obvious in activities other than reading or spelling – reproducing sequences of mixed letters; in spelling; when attempting to read individual words?
- Does the child have poor co-ordination at either the fine or gross level, or both?
- Does the child have low motivation?
- Is the child hyperactive?
- Does the child have low self-esteem and a poor self-image, possibly combined with other secondary emotional problems caused by constant failure in school with little or no academic progress?

Advice for supporting children with dyslexia in mainstream classrooms will often come from specialists from outside the school, although, in cases where children are clearly dyslexic, but the problem is not considered to be of sufficient magnitude to be granted outside assessment or support, teachers need to plan and use particular approaches for themselves.

It is almost a given that advice for teaching children who have dyslexia is based on good teaching practice, and would be of benefit to most children in a class. If at all possible, the teacher should:

- use clear and neat handwriting;
- limit the amount of copying from a board that is required;
- provide word lists when new topics are first introduced;
- give enough time for writing down such things as homework, not just the final seconds of a lesson;
- repeat instructions or questions clearly;
- stress patterns and similarities in words and sounds and take every opportunity to draw attention to the application of spelling rules.

It is worth repeating that all of the above might be considered as good practice whether catering for pupils with or without dyslexia.

The following list of advice for teachers should be seen as a set of possible starting points that could be developed as routines. Most of them, again, are equally applicable for all teaching situations. Although they would probably need to be followed more precisely, and given more importance and prominence for children with dyslexia, if they are to be of greatest benefit to them.

■ Nothing should be assumed: reading, writing, spelling and maths skills should be taught thoroughly, and, in many cases, repeatedly and not left to chance.

■ It is best to practise skills in a meaningful and, if possible, authentic way so that they are used in a more real context, rather than carrying out endless drills and exercises. If possible, children should be encouraged to read and write for real purposes (see Chapter 3).

■ Read every day. This should include the teacher reading to the child while they follow the words, and the child reading to the teacher (adult) with appropriate support ('prompt–pause–praise'; see below).

■ Reading skills are best taught in context (this relates to what we have considered earlier, in Chapter 3).

■ Provide as much interesting and stimulating reading material as possible; find out what will interest the child.

■ In your classroom, try to create an environment where reading is enjoyable and relaxing. This is of benefit to all learners.

■ Be sure to use praise effectively, but judiciously. Over praising can have detrimental effects.

■ Pay extra attention to the teaching of sound–symbol correspondence and word-building (see 'over-teaching', below).

■ Try to teach and reinforce a few simple spelling rules.

■ Teach letter formation and handwriting in parallel with reading.

■ Use multisensory approaches, such as finger-tracing, plastic letters and saying at the same time as writing.

■ If possible, allow time for intensive and regular individual sessions. They should be well targeted, focusing on specific difficulties and using multisensory and over-teaching methods.

■ Involve parents in supporting children with practice tasks and other homework.

■ Be sure that all colleagues are aware of the individual problems being experienced.

Specific language impairment

Specific language impairment (SLI) is a term that covers a range of difficulties associated with learning and using language. The particular difficulties covered by this umbrella term are not usually linked with general learning difficulties (see above), nor are they linked with any of the conditions that we will consider later, such as autistic spectrum disorders, attention-deficit/hyperactivity disorder, Down's or other syndromes, or with cerebral palsy. SLI is not linked specifically with hearing impairments. Children who have been diagnosed with SLI are no less intelligent than others in their age cohort, and yet they have significant difficulty with speech and language; their difficulties are 'specific' to this particular area.

Difficulty with speech and language arises when a child does not follow the usual pattern of development as far as speech and language generally are concerned. Cases of SLI are more widespread than is generally taken into account by those faced with pupils who are experiencing developmental difficulties in class; indeed, the incidence of SLI is reported to be more prevalent than autistic spectrum disorders, for example. The incidence of SLI in very young children is estimated to be 7 per cent (Tomblin *et al.* 1997) compared with an estimate of 0.9 per cent for children with an autistic spectrum disorder (see below) (Green 2005).

A child exhibiting SLI is often, but not exclusively, of average or above average intelligence, but, despite this, they have great difficulty in understanding the language, in its broadest sense, that they are confronted with in the daily routines of school and life generally. For example, despite having good ideas, which they could contribute orally, it is not possible for them to construct sentences that will adequately convey what they mean, or what they want to say. Children in this situation do not have any other recognised condition, such as some of those described in this chapter, which might account for their difficulty.

The causes of SLI are not understood, and one of its features is that it can present itself differently in different individuals, which makes it difficult to diagnose effectively. What has been established is that the speech and language centres of the brain do not develop as would be expected, despite there being no clear indication as to why, and that there seems to be a genetic link, with the condition passing from a parent to children. As with many of the psychological conditions that can affect children's progress with learning, there is not a definitive test that can be used as a tool for diagnosis. For this reason, the condition is often left undiagnosed.

'Specific language impairment' is actually one of three terms that can often be found in the literature, and also in more common use. The other two are 'developmental delay', and 'developmental language disorder'. In each case, the term refers to children who have significant problems with their grasp of, and facility with, spoken language. The term 'specific language impairment' is the one used most widely, and it is only applied to children whose difficulties are not the result of any other underlying intellectual, psychological or environmental consideration.

For a child with this condition, it is likely that they will:

- give every impression of understanding what is being said, but it is not possible, or, at least, very difficult, to understand what the child is attempting to say;

- speak clearly and will speak at length, in many cases, but fail to get the point of a conversation, often making inappropriate comments and responses that fail to make sense to the listener;
- be able to speak readily and understandably in single words, but not manage to link single words together in a way that forms coherent sentences; often, words are simply omitted.

In extreme cases, they will:

- understand virtually no spoken language and say very few words.

Often, a distinction between comprehension (understanding language) and expression (using language) is made when considering SLI. Most children who have an SLI are likely to be better accomplished in one area, though they may have difficulties in both. The areas can be grouped as follows:

- *Concerning speech apparatus*: that is, the mouth, tongue, nose, breathing and how these elements are co-ordinated and operated by muscles; children with a difficulty in this area only are usually identified quickly as having a speech and language impairment.
- *Concerning phonology*: that is, the sounds that go together to make up language.
- *Concerning syntax (grammar and morphology)*: that is, the way that words and parts of words combine to make phrases and sentences.
- *Concerning semantics*: that is, the meaning of words, parts of words and phrases and sentences.
- *Concerning pragmatics*: that is, how we use language in different situations and how we convey feelings.
- *Concerning intonation and stress (prosody)*: that is, the rhythms and inflections of the way we speak.

A child with difficulties in any or all of these areas will, naturally, have difficulty with comprehension, expression or, more likely, with both. A child may have difficulties other than the one that is most obvious. As would be expected, a considerable level of expertise is needed to assess a child with a suspected SLI.

Pragmatic language impairment

Formerly referred to as 'semantic pragmatic disorder', one of the manifestations of SLI is 'pragmatic language impairment'. This will be explored here as one example of an SLI. Pragmatic language impairment is a disorder leading to an inability to fully process and understand language. It is thought to be associated with autism, since the elements of the triad (which is considered later) of communication, imagination and socialising are, in many cases, the focus of the problems. Pragmatic language impairment is sometimes described as the 'outer spectrum of autism'. As children with any level of autism are likely to display the difficulties associated with it, it is sometimes difficult for a wholly accurate diagnosis to be made. Children with pragmatic language impairment often behave in a markedly different way in different social settings; most notably, at home and at school. For this reason, it is important that reports from parents of behaviour that is in keeping with any possibility of pragmatic language impairment, or any of the other related disorders, are accepted as accurate and therefore taken seriously.

Children with this problem can sound very grown up, but often the detail of what they say is imprecise or difficult to understand for others. Some of the following may be present:

- difficulties giving specific information about a particular event;
- little or no eye contact;
- poor understanding of abstract concepts (e.g. guessing; the future);
- not asking for help from teachers;
- not inviting others to play with them;
- coming across as rude or arrogant;
- late reading development or, conversely, early reading development, but usually with very limited understanding of what they read;
- not good at team games, or co-operating generally;
- anxiety about large groups or crowds;
- not good in social situations (e.g. break-times or children's parties);
- problems with motor skills (e.g. writing, drawing, riding a bike, tying laces);
- very easily distracted in noisy or busy situations.

To help children overcome the problems that make learning difficult, it helps to try and provide the following:

- practical, hands-on tasks;
- a quiet, working environment;
- visual clues to support understanding;
- routines giving predictability to their day;
- small groups;
- good role models in socialising;
- simple instructions given slowly;
- carefully composed language (e.g. say 'put your books into the box', not 'clear up');
- allowing additional time for a reply when asked a question;
- model answers to questions (e.g. replying for them);
- clear rules on how to behave, using concrete language they can understand;
- constant positive reminders supported by visual/written information;
- clearly written instructions (e.g. timetable, instructions for current task, messages home).

When listening to children with this condition, it is helpful to try and respond to their intended message, if it can be decoded, rather than what is actually said, as this may not always make sense. Children with pragmatic language impairment do not, in general, understand sarcasm, metaphors or jokes, but, when these things arise, it is helpful to explain them.

Autistic spectrum disorders

Autism is a condition of more or less unknown cause, which can mean that the individuals who are most severely affected are isolated, uncommunicative and wholly unsociable. In severe cases, it appears that there is no link between the mind of the individual and the immediate environment of the social context where they are placed. This can be extremely disturbing for those around them.

In itself, autism does not imply a particular learning difficulty. Many children with autism and related conditions learn perfectly well, and many are of high intelligence. However, the nature of autism, as we will see, means that it can be incredibly difficult for those with the condition to operate in conventional classrooms and under usual learning conditions.

Autism was first described in 1912 by the Swiss psychiatrist Paul (Eugen) Bleuler. The word derives from '*autos*' (self) and '*ismos*' (state), and implies an over-exaggerated concern with oneself and little for the environment or for others. The defining characteristics of autism are summed up by what is referred to as a 'triad of impairment'. This terminology was first used by Wing and Gould (1979), but see also NAS (2008). The triad focuses on communication, imagination and socialisation.

- *Communication*: language is impaired across all modes of communication, which includes speech, intonation, gesture, facial expression and other body language.
- *Imagination*: thought processes are rigid and inflexible, and this is manifested by a resistance to change and obsessional, even ritualistic, behaviours.
- *Socialisation*: any relationships are extremely problematic, social timing is poor and there is a lack of social empathy, normal body contact is shunned, and eye contact is rare or inappropriate.

Autism – definition

Autism is a developmental disorder characterised by severe deficits in social interaction and communication, by an obsession with an extremely limited range of activities and interests, and, often, by the presence of repetitive behaviours. Those with autism are often excessively rigid in their behaviour and response to stimuli, and are largely emotionally detached.

Children with the most extreme version of autism are not able to socialise enough for them to be educated in mainstream schools. However, there is a wide range of severity within the realm of autism, and, for this reason, the condition is described by means of a spectrum, with mild autism at one end of a continuum and extreme autism at the other. One of the most commonly encountered disorders on the autistic spectrum is Asperger's syndrome.

Asperger's syndrome

Since Asperger's syndrome is a disorder on the autistic spectrum, those who have the condition will have restrictions to normal functioning in communication, in socialisation, in imagination. They will lack, to lesser or greater extents, the ability to behave and think with any flexibility, and, often, they will have poor physical co-ordination. It affects both boys and girls, but boys are affected in significantly greater numbers. The condition was originally described by Hans Asperger, an Austrian psychiatrist, in 1944.

Asperger's syndrome is a very individual condition, and, although it is not correct to say that all cases will be different, there is a wide variation both in severity and in specific manifestations. As with all autistic spectrum disorders, there are wide variations in the physical and mental symptoms, and in the degree of difficulty that these present.

The characteristics of Asperger's syndrome can be summarised as follows:

- Children with Asperger's syndrome are sometimes described as having 'high-functioning autism', but the two are usually diagnosed as separate conditions.

- Often, there is no significant language delay during the early years.

- Children with Asperger's syndrome are usually of average or above intelligence and can have good verbal skills. Sometimes, the content of what they say may be abnormal; for example, lengthy discussions on a favourite subject.

- There is a tendency to take literal meaning – for example, 'hop into bed' – and an inability to read body language and facial expressions. Subtlety in humour is not usually understood.

- Little use of facial expression is made and the use of gestures may be limited. Speech and intonation can be monotonous.

- Children with Asperger's syndrome often have poor physical and visual motor skills; clumsiness and poor co-ordination are also characteristic, although there are cases where these difficulties are not particularly obvious.

- Children with Asperger's syndrome usually have a narrow range of interests and become very knowledgeable on their chosen specialism, often to the exclusion of everything else. They often adhere to a set of specific rituals, and often show a distinct lack of flexibility or imagination.

- Children with Asperger's syndrome often have excellent memories, especially for recall in rote fashion.

- Children with Asperger's syndrome do not like change. They have routines which they are comfortable with and resist any form of change.

- Children with Asperger's syndrome are able to work towards adapting to social situations, far more so than do those with autism. They have a desire to form social relationships, but have marked problems with interaction and understanding the unspoken rules of social behaviour.

- Children with Asperger's syndrome tend to be egotistical and opinionated – very unhelpful in social situations.

- Often, pronounced anxiety is a feature of the condition, centring on low self-esteem and fear of failure, as well as a fear of being misunderstood and of not understanding others. Anxiety is often a result of self-awareness; in particular, with being different and of not fitting in to their immediate social circle.

Problems experienced by those with Asperger's syndrome

Children with Asperger's syndrome often appear to be coping with their academic work in primary school, although there is a significant proportion who do not make good progress. They are often extremely anxious and usually have few, or no, friends. Disruptive behaviour, often born out of frustration and anxiety, can be a feature of their conduct either at home or at school – or, in some cases, both. For some children, the transfer from primary to secondary school, or some other similar disruption to routine, can be the point where problems become more apparent or difficult to deal with. At secondary school, the difficulties are not always necessarily to do with academic work. The problems are more likely to be a result of not being able to understand the unspoken signals and intentions from those around them. There is also often difficulty with understanding the meaning of the instructions given in lessons. The inability to interpret and act upon the mix of verbal and non-verbal language used by teachers and other pupils presents obvious difficulties, particularly if it leads to work not being completed, or apparent disobedience. There is an increased possibility of bullying, owing to their lack of social skills and their reactions to unfamiliar or misunderstood situations. The implications of Asperger's syndrome are widespread in all social settings, but they are often more pronounced in school as the child does not have the option of not attending.

Dealing with autistic spectrum disorders in the classroom

With children who are clearly on the autistic spectrum, it is important to realise that they will not respond in the same way as other children when dealing with the day-to-day affairs of the classroom. Whereas some children would respond well to a raised eyebrow or a shake of the head if they are in the process of doing something that they should not be doing, an autistic child will not understand, or even notice, this subtlety of body language. Neither are they likely to respond well to a raised voice, or even a quieter 'telling off' – they will simply not understand what is happening. In order to be able to begin to deal with children of this nature, it is important, first, to bear in mind that they are different and will respond very differently from the other children in your class, and, second, to remember that children on the autistic spectrum are all individually different as well. For this reason, it is best to spend more time than might be normal in getting to know them and attempting to work out the sorts of approaches that are likely to be successful – and, possibly more importantly, those that will not be successful.

The Education and Training Inspectorate (ETI) of the Department of Education, Northern Ireland (DENI) have produced a booklet, 'Autistic spectrum disorders: a guide to classroom practice'(Hunter 2006), which gives a set of principles that are useful for those dealing, perhaps for the first time, with children with autism or Asperger's syndrome. The following advice is derived mainly from this source.

- It is important to get to know the child as an individual, and to try to understand the particular manifestation of their condition and to learn about how it affects learning.
- Use the child's strengths to teach new skills; attention to detail, for example.
- Give the child an opportunity to explain a situation from their point of view; this may well give an unexpected insight into the child's view of the topic.
- Try to reduce the amount of language you use when giving instructions. Keep the instructions clear, simple and direct.
- Give the child enough time to process information, rather than expecting an immediate response.
- When speaking, try to avoid idioms; they can be confusing and are likely to be taken literally.
- Give instructions positively. Explain what should be done, rather than what should not be done.
- Work with routines and simple structures.
- When setting targets, be sure that they are realistic and attainable; work with short-term targets rather than those that may continue for a longer period.
- Create opportunities for independence and social interaction.
- Teach social skills, as they do not come naturally; even simple things like saying 'Thank you'.
- If a child has a teaching assistant, it will help the child's self-esteem if the assistant is seen working with other pupils.
- Be aware that usual strategies for calming a child may not work. The child may need time alone rather than being comforted by another person.

- Keep all staff informed of the strategies you are using as consistency is very important.

- Have regular contact with parents. This is useful in terms of consistency of approach.

Many of the points above, as we saw with strategies for supporting children with dyslexia, would be of value to many children. For example, not using abstract language or unusual idiomatic phrases, or giving time for a child to formulate a response to a question and not assuming either that they cannot answer or that they are being lazy or disobedient.

Attention-deficit/hyperactivity disorder

Attention deficit disorder with or without hyperactivity disorder is a condition in which, when compared with most children of the same age and sex, the child has a range of behavioural problems associated with poor attention span and concentration. These problems include:

- pronounced inattentiveness;

- pronounced impulsiveness (not thinking before saying or doing something);

- restlessness;

- hyperactivity (being unable to control the amount of physical activity that is appropriate to a particular situation);

- underdeveloped learning and social skills.

Any one of the above would be a cause for concern, but, when they are combined and pronounced, they lead to some very challenging situations for teachers, and often for other members of the class or school, not to mention the family. When the resultant symptoms (listed below) are combined with the symptoms of hyperactivity and the combination condition of ADHD (as attention-deficit/hyperactivity disorder is also commonly known) is present, the problems for all involved are increased. It should be noted that the problems are not just for those around the child – teachers, parents and peers – but also for the child. It can be difficult being unable to conform to the expectations of adults and other children, and this is likely to lead to other problems; in particular, those associated with poor self-esteem.

Children with attention deficit disorder are likely to exhibit some, or all, of the following:

- They do not pay close attention to detail and make careless, avoidable errors in their work.

- They consistently fail to finish tasks.

- They appear not to be listening.

- They do not follow instructions, or follow them only partially.

- They are disorganised.

- They avoid tasks requiring sustained mental effort.
- They lose things (e.g. pencils, books, toys).
- They are very easily distracted.
- They are forgetful.

Children with problems with hyperactivity are likely to exhibit some, or all, of the following:

- They run around and climb over things unnecessarily.
- They are excessively noisy and unable to take part in quiet activities.
- They are unable to stay in a seat.
- They fidget constantly.

Children with pronounced impulsiveness often exhibit some, or all, of the following:

- They shout out answers.
- They fail to wait in lines or take turns.
- They constantly interrupt the conversations or the games of others.
- They talk excessively without considering others.

Added to the list above, children with ADHD are likely to have temper tantrums, sleep disorders, clumsiness, general behaviour problems, specific learning difficulties, depression and anxiety disorders.

To help children with this condition, teachers or other adults, including those in parental roles, need to provide clear structures and routines linked with a dogged consistency. Rules need to be clearly and simply defined and supported by structured sanctions and rewards. Deliberate and sustained eye contact when speaking to the children is often helpful in keeping their attention – and, above all, there is a need for an enormous amount of patience.

There is no doubt that children with ADHD are difficult and challenging to deal with, both at home and at school. They need to be in a structured environment so that they have fewer problems with starting and completing tasks, moving from place to place and from task to task, working with others, following instructions and maintaining attention. They need predictability, structure, short work periods, more individual instruction, positive reinforcement and an interesting curriculum, all of which, as we have seen earlier with the case of dyslexia, are examples of good classroom practice and would benefit all learners. In the case of those with ADHD, though, they are even more important.

If possible, teachers should try to:

- remember that the child's behaviour is not intentionally naughty;
- have positive expectations;

- provide clear and frequently repeated instructions;

- provide regular feedback and praise (when appropriate);

- make use of clear and understandable rules in the classroom, which are set out in a positive framework (what should be done, not what should not);

- provide reminders in the form of lists and sets of instructions that the child can access themselves, either when necessary or when reminded;

- repeat instructions, possibly in different formats – written, spoken, even visual, and check for understanding;

- make clear and deliberate, even over-exaggerated, eye contact when speaking to the children;

- not be drawn into long explanations of right and wrong in their behaviour (simply tell the children what you want, in a positive mode);

- not expect the children to complete lengthy tasks, especially for homework;

- provide time away from the classroom, if possible, when stress levels rise;

- work towards making their work enjoyable and avoiding potential boredom (as for all children);

- exhibit consistency, firmness, fairness and patience.

Other conditions that affect learning

There are many other conditions and syndromes that have an effect on the progress of children's learning. Some of them are severe and would not, under normal circumstances, be experienced in mainstream schools. We will briefly mention a few of them here.

Down's syndrome

Down's syndrome is a genetically caused condition in which the individual has 47 chromosomes instead of the usual 46. For the majority of people with Down's syndrome, there is no specific reason for this. However, its incidence does increase slightly with the mother's age. For every 1,000 babies born, there will be one with Down's syndrome. This means that there are about 600 children with Down's syndrome born each year in the UK (DSA 2013). There is no treatment or cure for Down's syndrome, but it is hoped that advances in genetic science may eventually provide something to help, if not cure or prevent, it.

Down's syndrome is considered to be the most common cause of learning difficulties. Children with Down's syndrome usually meet the developmental expectations that other children meet, but generally some months or even years later. In the past, those with Down's syndrome often did not live beyond the age of 20 to 30, but it is now the case, as a result of advances in care procedures, that many live for nearly as long, on average, as the general population.

Children with Down's syndrome have moderate learning difficulties, and, as we have observed, their all-round general development is somewhat delayed compared with that of their peers. They are generally very happy, fit and healthy, although they are sometimes more prone to coughs and colds than others. They are also prone to heart problems, hearing problems and thyroid disease as they get older.

A child who has Down's syndrome will have some distinctive physical features, but some children who share some of these features will not have the syndrome. The common physical features of Down's syndrome are:

- delayed growth (small for age);
- eyes that slant to some degree;
- slightly flattened nose and face;
- small mouth, but larger than normal tongue, which can lead to the tongue protruding (this can be minimised by training);
- poor muscle tone.

Cerebral palsy

'Cerebral palsy' is a term covering a number of disorders affecting muscles, movement and mobility. It occurs when the part of the brain controlling movement is either damaged in some way or has failed to develop properly. In the case of underdevelopment, this may be present from birth. There is no one identifiable cause of cerebral palsy, but it is thought that a virus, certain drug use by the mother, poor nutrition or premature birth may be contributory factors. Also implicated are low birth weight, poor supply of oxygen around the time of birth, or injury to the brain before, during or just after the birth. Early childhood meningitis or encephalitis, diseases affecting the brain or its lining, can also cause the condition. There are approximately 1,800 babies diagnosed with cerebral palsy in Britain each year.

The physical characteristics of those with cerebral palsy include some, but certainly not all, of the following:

- limited or uncontrolled movements;
- poor mobility;
- muscle weakness and/or stiffness;
- muscle spasm or 'floppiness';
- problems with speech;
- hearing difficulties;
- visual difficulties;

- difficulties chewing and swallowing food;
- a tendency towards epilepsy.

All of the above can lead to certain difficulties in learning, but there is no indication that those with cerebral palsy are any less intelligent than others. In extreme cases, difficulties with communication can be an obstacle to learning.

Conduct disorder

Conduct disorder is a little known, though not rare, condition. It affects 6.5 per cent of boys and 2.7 per cent of girls between the ages of 5 and 10 (Richardson and Joughin 2002). It has, for some time, been officially defined in the USA, and recently, in 2013, was listed by the National Institute for Health and Clinical Excellence (NIHCE) in the UK as a recognisable condition.

Conduct disorder (also known as CD) – and oppositional defiant disorder (ODD), the term often used when very young children display symptoms of conduct disorder in the home – is a psychological disorder diagnosed in childhood, and which presents itself as a repetitive and persistent pattern of behaviour in which the basic rights of others, or some of the norms of behaviour for a particular age group, are grossly violated. These behaviours are often referred to as 'antisocial behaviours'. Indeed, the disorder is often seen as the precursor to antisocial personality disorder.

Naturally, there are times when children behave badly, and children are known to go through phases in which their behaviour can vary markedly. It is well established that very young children and adolescents alike can be particularly challenging from time to time; however, most of them will develop into well-behaved and well-adjusted members of society at large.

Children's tantrums, or occasional incidents of aggressive behaviour, can, for the most part, be viewed as being within the broad pattern of normal development, or as children showing their occasional frustrations in an angry or defiant manner. But, if a child continually behaves badly for very long periods (months rather than days or weeks), and if they are consistently and repeatedly very badly behaved as well as being aggressive and destructive, there may be cause for concern. In cases defined within the range for conduct disorder to be considered, the patterns of behaviour in question will be very much outside of the normal range of what can be expected – and tolerated. The behaviour will consistently breech the accepted rules applied in schools and in the home, and, when witnessed, it will clearly be beyond what teachers, parents and others can reasonably be expected to manage. It is the sort of behaviour that will be seriously detrimental to the child's general development, and also detrimental to the general well being, and even mental health, of those around them. In school, whole classes can be disrupted, while, at home, parents and siblings can be placed under extreme stress.

The possible manifestations of conduct disorder include children being involved in violent physical fights, and they may be guilty of repeated stealing or lying. Children in this situation do not show any of guilt or remorse when they have been discovered and confronted. They will not adhere to rules or codes of conduct that are specifically agreed for them to follow, and they may also become involved in illegal activities. Often, truancy will be a feature of their behaviour, and, as they grow older, they are likely to stay out all night.

There is not a single known cause of conduct disorder, but there is a growing understanding of the possible multiple causes. Conduct disorder (or oppositional defiant disorder) is potentially likely to develop if a child:

- has particular genes for antisocial behaviour;
- has had difficulty with learning acceptable social behaviour;
- has an existing learning difficulty;
- suffers from depression;
- has experienced bullying or has been abused;
- is 'hyperactive', possibly diagnosed with ADHD;
- comes from a family background with poor parenting, including discipline problems and general lack of family organisation.

A young child with the initial signs of conduct disorder is most likely to be male, to have ADHD and to be of low general intelligence. As with many problems and disorders, early diagnosis and intervention can give better chances of future improvement. Intervention is sometimes offered in the home, or, later, at school or within the local child health organisational structure, such as the local child and adolescent mental health service. It is considered essential that the family is wholly involved in the process of treatment.

Treatment for the extreme behavioural problems associated with conduct disorder is usually centred around helping the child to work on positive social behaviour, and on working towards the control of antisocial and destructive behaviour. Naturally, this can be a long and difficult process.

Children who have conduct disorder find school very trying, experiencing constant difficulties with confrontation and punishment of one sort or another. Teachers, and others in schools, should also be working towards reinforcing positive behaviour in support of the work that is carried out at home and with other professionals. Close liaison and co-operation is, clearly, very important.

Programmes to deliver improved social skills are sometimes implemented jointly at home and at school. Individual support in the classroom and around school generally is also something that is provided. In extreme cases, children are placed in special educational settings such as referral units, or in schools that specialise in dealing with such problems.

Obsessive–compulsive disorder

Obsessive–compulsive disorder is a common, treatable, neuropsychiatric disorder. (A neuropsychiatric disorder is one of a wide range of neurological conditions, which includes depression, anxiety, Tourette's syndrome (described later), alcohol and drug dependence, post-traumatic stress disorder and some sleep disorders.) Obsessive–compulsive disorder is recognised in those suffering by their excessive, intrusive and inappropriate obsessions (defined as uninvited thoughts that occur over and over again) and compulsions (defined as repetitive, often pointless or senseless actions that they have to perform, which can be physical or mental actions). Those with obsessive–compulsive disorder have no control whatsoever over their obsessions and compulsions. They appear without warning and will not disappear simply by the will of the sufferer. The causes of obsessive–compulsive disorder are not fully understood, but it is fairly clear that it is not the fault of the sufferer in any way; nor is it the result of a dysfunctional personality or family situation. There is a possibility that there is a genetic connection, as it is known to run in families.

Obsessive–compulsive disorder is more common than is often realised. It is estimated that approximately 1.2 per cent of adults in Britain currently suffer from it, and it is reasonable to assume that there are many more unreported cases.

Obsessive–compulsive disorder is predominantly an adult mental health condition, but it is estimated that 1 in 100 children have the condition in some form, although this is usually in a mild form. Obsessive–compulsive behaviours can be extreme and disabling, but this is not always the case. Sometimes, the obsessions or compulsions are relatively mild and can act as a reassurance. Such things as kissing when leaving someone, having a bedtime routine, including a story, can be supportive and reassuring. When the rituals are overbearing and persistent, when they are clearly pointless (such as having to touch all of the mirrors in a house before leaving, even in a set order), when they lead to anxiety or distress or when leading a more or less normal life becomes impossible (often, this impossibility is for those around the sufferer), there is a need for professional help. This help might be in the form of cognitive behaviour therapy, medication or a combination of the two.

This condition may not always interfere with learning. This depends, first, upon its severity, and, second, upon the nature of the obsessions or compulsions. An example of an interference might be a compulsion with perfection and neatness. There have been cases of schoolchildren copying out entire pieces of work, or even the entire content of an exercise book, because of a minor error made near the end. Other obsessive behaviour can relate to starting conditions for carrying out work and can be extreme to the point where no work is actually completed. Lower-level behaviours can include nail biting or other grooming activities. Some of the common obsessions and compulsions are: a fear of contamination with dirt, germs or poison; the need for symmetry of actions or events (e.g. if I touch the door handle with my left hand, I must also touch it with my right hand); repetitive checking actions; repeatedly saying something either out loud or internally; checking and re-checking that doors and windows are locked; excessive and repetitive hand washing, cleaning, counting or hoarding; touching objects or people; being excessively precise; constantly asking for reassurance.

Attachment disorder

When children fail, for any variety of reasons, to develop secure attachments with those caring for them during their early years (typically, birth to 3 years old), they are likely to develop attachment disorder. If a child's principal requirements for food, water, love, comfort and security are not met, or are provided inconsistently, a level of anxiety develops concerning the possibility of their future and immediate needs not being met, and a strong and general mistrust for all people develops. The child begins to centre their thoughts and actions exclusively and often aggressively on themselves and their needs, to the exclusion of any feelings towards others. They have an overbearing need to take control of everything around them and to reject approaches, of any sort, by any person.

The nature of the child's behaviour makes it very difficult for anyone to form a relationship with them. This includes teachers, who will be mistrusted and, at best, disliked. This will lead to clear and obvious difficulties in teaching and, therefore, in learning. The child is likely to reject any offer of support, or refuse to undertake any of the routine learning activities provided in school. In extreme cases, the child will be considered unteachable, although it is often the case that they will co-operate at some times but not at others.

Children with attachment disorder often have the following characteristics – usually, not all of them and in varying degrees:

- They can be charming and engaging, but on a very superficial level.
- They avoid eye contact.
- They can be overly and indiscriminately affectionate with people not known to them.
- They can be extremely uncomfortable when affection is offered to them and are unable to show affection to others.
- They are often very difficult to control. They become involved in antisocial and personally destructive behaviour such as stealing within the family, or solvent abuse.
- They can be destructive to themselves and to others, or their property.
- They are unable to show kindness of any sort to pets.
- They are likely to lie, often unnecessarily.
- They are often unable to control impulses.
- They are often unable to think through the effects of their actions.
- They appear to have no conscience, consequently not understanding guilt or remorse.
- Their relations with peers or siblings are extremely problematic.
- They are likely to ask pointless and meaningless questions and to constantly talk at inappropriate times.

- They can be excessively and inappropriately demanding.
- They can be passively aggressive, often attempting to provoke a reaction from others.
- They can give the impression of unexpected maturity for their age.
- They often have low self-esteem and a poor self-image.
- They can exhibit the signs of repressed anger.
- They are capable of disrupting, even destroying, events or placements such as family gatherings, foster arrangements or school.

These children are very difficult to deal with, but, with appropriate, well-planned approaches, there are good possibilities for improvement. Dealing with the problem is not something that a school can attempt alone. With strong professional support for the child, family and school, children with attachment disorder can eventually come to learn that adults are to be trusted and that the world can be safe. It can be a long journey, but, with consistent responses from adults, including teachers, over an extended period, improvement with relationships can be made.

Fragile X syndrome

Fragile X is probably the most common form of inherited learning disability. It is caused by a gene defect in the X chromosome. The condition is often passed from one generation to the next. It can be present in boys and girls alike; however, it is twice as common in boys (approximately 1 in 4,000). The range of learning difficulties that it can lead to are various, and can be from mild to severe. In most cases, the effects on boys are more severe than on girls. This is probably because girls have two X chromosomes, and the unaffected one may in some way be able to compensate for the deficiency in the other.

Difficulties for the children affected can be summarised under three headings: cognitive, physical and behavioural.

1 *Cognitive*: The range of abilities of these children is wide. Most boys with Fragile X will have some form of learning disability, which can range from mild to severe. Girls are affected less in most cases.

2 *Physical*: The physical features of Fragile X are usually fairly subtle, and can go unnoticed. Some people with Fragile X may have heads that are larger than average, sometimes with long faces and large jaws; there are also possibilities of protruding ears, high palates and teeth that are overcrowded.

3 *Behavioural*: Those with Fragile X can display many features in common with autism; for example, anxiety in crowded or noisy places or a dislike of direct eye contact. Those with Fragile X are relaxed with the routines with which they are familiar, but find change difficult. They tend to be happy in company and certainly do not, usually, avoid social situations. The main problems are centred on impulsivity, poor attention and hyperactivity, particularly in boys.

They sometimes have poor motor control and difficulties with speech and language. Their speech may be repetitive, making use of learnt phrases over and over again.

Williams syndrome

Williams syndrome is a relatively uncommon genetic condition that causes both physical and mental disabilities. It is caused by a gene deficiency in the gene that controls the production of elastin, a protein important for heart and artery development and for controlling the function of the heart. It is often difficult to confirm the condition and it may go undiagnosed for many years. Those with Williams syndrome have characteristic facial features that become more pronounced as the child grows. Children with Williams syndrome will show overall developmental delay and learning difficulties ranging from mild to quite severe, although some have very good memories. Children with Williams syndrome, in general, tend to:

- be excessively anxious or fearful;
- have a short attention span;
- display obsessive behaviours;
- be hyperactive;
- be overly friendly, displaying no shyness of strangers;
- have low-pitched voices;
- have delayed language development;
- be small for their age;
- have very well-developed hearing;
- have poor communication skills.

Tourette's syndrome

Tourette's syndrome is a neuropsychiatric disorder (see above) characterised by a range of tics, which are sudden, spasmodic, painless and involuntary muscular contractions that often affect the face; they also, most characteristically, have vocal tics. There is no definitive cause identified for Tourette's syndrome, but, in approximately half of all cases, there is a hereditary connection of some kind. Tourette's syndrome often starts first in primary school, but becomes far more apparent, and far more of a problem, between the ages of 10 and 14. The severity of the tics changes from day to day. The reason for this is not fully understood, although it might be related to stress. Boys are more likely to be affected than girls. Many people with Tourette's syndrome have a measure of control over their tics, but in many cases, when the conscious control is relaxed, they become more frequent and pronounced. The condition often improves with the onset of adolescence. The tics, which are sometimes described as 'twitches', can cause distress for those affected. They are often teased by those around them, especially in school.

The most common tics are:

- coughing and throat clearing;
- grunting;
- spitting;
- swearing;
- stammering;
- hissing;
- shouting;
- eye blinking or eye rolling;
- squinting;
- nose twitching;
- lip smacking;
- shoulder shrugging;
- arm raising.

Tourette's syndrome is associated with autistic spectrum disorders, eating disorders and sensory sensitivity. About three-quarters of children with Tourette's syndrome also have some signs of attention deficit and hyperactivity. Others are dyslexic and/or dyspraxic. Approximately half are known to suffer from obsessive–compulsive disorder, and also to suffer from anxieties and phobias. Other symptoms can include moodiness, echolalia (repeating the words of others), echopraxia (mimicking the actions of others), palilalia (repeating internal words or thoughts), coprolalia (swearing and using other obscene language), speech atypicalities (unusual rhythms, tone, accents, loudness and very rapid speech), copropraxia (making obscene gestures), stuttering and, in extreme cases, self-harming behaviour (such things as cutting, scratching, head banging and eye poking).

Young people with Tourette's syndrome often lose their temper quickly, and often over react in unexpected situations. They have difficulties with impulsivity, and are often defiant. They tend to have problems organising their schoolwork, sitting quietly, playing and knowing when and when not it is appropriate to speak. They often interrupt others, or bother them by taking over their workspace. They do not listen to the teacher and they are often extremely disorganised, losing their work, books, pens and pencils. They some-times undertake dangerous activities – climbing, jumping and so on – without concern for their safety or the safety of others.

One approach to dealing with the problems associated with vocal tics in the classroom is referred to as 'planned ignorance'. It amounts to ignoring the tics and relies on the teacher explaining to the class and providing a role model for dealing with the situation. It is vital, in a case like this, that everyone in the class is made aware of the nature of Tourette's syndrome and that the noises are unintentional and largely unavoidable. The reason for this approach is that, when a person with Tourette's syndrome knows that vocal tics are more unacceptable in certain situations, it is far more likely that they will occur in that situation. This is partly a function of increased stress. The partial acceptance that is implicit in the planned ignorance approach reduces stress, which can lead to fewer vocal outbursts. Time away from the classroom can also reduce stress. Even a short trip to the toilet can calm the situation down.

Summary

We have seen that there are many reasons why the path of learning is not always a smooth one, and we have considered some of the causes and some of the reasons, which can have a formal diagnosis.

Most learning difficulties have their roots in either inherited conditions or genetic faults, problems at or around birth, or later injury, abuse or other environmental factors. So-called 'impairments' might be physical, sensory or intellectual and affect one or more of the four stages of intellectual activity, namely:

1 *input*: the process of taking in and recording information that has been received via the senses;

2 *integration*: the process whereby information is interpreted, categorised, placed in sequence and linked with previous learning;

3 *memory*: the stage where information is placed into storage for later retrieval and use;

4 *output*: the time when actions are taken based on the processing of stored information; this can be in the form of language or of action (e.g. movements or gestures).

Of the most common problems likely to be encountered in mainstream classrooms (as opposed to the problems common in special schools or units), dyslexia looms large and has, in recent years, become better understood. Approaches to teaching children with dyslexia have improved, and are still improving. There is a range of measures that teachers can take to help learning potential to be reached, in a way that has not hitherto been possible. The fact that dyslexia is far more widely recognised as a real and diagnosable condition (albeit very different in form and intensity from child to child) has helped teachers to be able to find out more about it and how to deal with it.

In the classroom

For teachers in classrooms, there are often limited resources and a limit to the available strategies for supporting children with particular difficulties. In many cases, the best support will come from outside the school. However, a teacher can, by taking an open and sensitive approach, and by finding out as much as possible about individual children, go some way towards alleviating some of the difficulties, knowing the child lies at the heart of effective support. However, this can be problematic, especially when the difficulties lead to unsuitable and even challenging classroom behaviour.

We should remember that many problems with bad behaviour have their roots in difficulties with learning. Unacceptable behaviour in the classroom and beyond is often born out of frustration, anger, fear or anxiety concerning what might be unnoticed, or perhaps only partially noticed; that is, difficulty with learning.

It is very important for teachers to avoid jumping to conclusions about the reasons for children behaving in certain ways. It is easy to decide that a child is lazy, uncooperative, rude, avoiding work by wandering about the room or by making 'funny' comments at inappropriate times, but, even in the midst of a stressful teaching situation, it is important to take time to consider the possible underlying causes of the behaviour. For some, this would be considered a weakness. They might say that 'good' teachers do not allow children to behave badly and instead ensure that they do the work expected of them. It is true that good teachers do keep good order in their classrooms and that they ensure that children complete the well-planned work that is expected of them – but good teachers also do a lot more than that. They are aware of the individual difficulties that their charges face and want to do something to help. This may sound too good to be true, but, in many cases, children will conform to expectations. Indeed, they are keen to conform to the teacher's expectations, and they will do so unless something overwhelming prevents them. An example of this, which may seem trivial in the context of the extreme difficulties that we have considered earlier, is the necessity to differentiate when planning work for children of different levels of ability and experience. Put simply, work that a teacher expects a child to complete must be at the appropriate level of difficulty for the child. The child must be capable of doing what is expected, sometimes with appropriate or scaffolded support (see Chapter 3). If the task is too easy, there is every likelihood that the child will not complete it (or complete it very quickly); if the task is too difficult, the child is very likely not to attempt to complete it; if the task is at a suitable level of difficulty (it is suitable for moving the child's understanding forward, across the zone of proximal development – see Chapter 3), there is a greatly increased chance that the child will get on and complete the work as expected. If children are not working on tasks set by the teacher, they will be perceived by the teacher as naughty, and, indeed, they may well choose to do something 'naughty' in place of the work set, but the underlying reason for not working is that they cannot do what is expected of them. This can be for one or more of a very large variety of reasons, as we have seen. This may not be a golden rule, but it is a reasonable picture of what can happen in classrooms.

A group of young children were asked to complete a labelling exercise on a sheet of paper that they had been given. They were told that they must write their full name on the sheet before doing anything else. This was stressed as being of great importance, and they were told that they must not start to label the items unless they had written their name in full. One boy was not capable of writing his full name. He wrote his first name and did no more. Forty minutes later, he was berated as lazy and told that he would miss his free time.

Perhaps he should have asked for help, in his own way; perhaps he should have moved on anyway; perhaps the teacher should have been aware of his problem and his reluctance to ask for help. But, in his mind, he was doing as he was told; he did not proceed to the labelling because he had not written his full name. Irrespective of his inability to write his full name, this scene shows that something has gone badly wrong. The child is branded as lazy, has suffered a blow to his self-esteem and the likelihood of him looking forward to school the next day has been seriously reduced.

Multisensory teaching

Multisensory teaching aims to involve the different senses in the process of learning. Multisensory teaching stresses the visual, auditory, oral and kinaesthetic systems of our bodies. Teachers make links between looking/seeing, listening/hearing and touching/feeling and combine many different experiences of the same idea or phenomenon by making use of different media and resources. Multisensory teaching approaches have been shown to be of particular value for children with reading and writing problems.

Over-teaching

This refers to the process of repeating the same or similar approaches to teaching a particular fact, concept or skill over a period of time until the learning is, or appears to be, sound. The repetition can be over a short time period, such as one lesson, or it might be a daily or weekly routine. The aim is to develop an automatic response and fix the item in question into long-term memory. It can be likened to some forms of behaviourist learning. (See Chapter 2.)

Look–say–cover–write–check

The look–say–cover–write–check is a support tool for learning spellings that makes use of a multisensory approach. Not only is it multisensory, but it is a prime example of engagement at both a conscious and unconscious level. The child has to actively work with the word and its letters, and has, unconsciously, to store it in short-term memory before reviewing it.

1 Select a word that needs to be learned.
2 Write the word clearly in lowercase letters.
3 Look at the word and focus on its shape.
4 Say it out loud, if possible, paying attention to the sounds.
5 Try to imagine the word as a picture in your mind.

6   Cover the word.

7   Straight away, write the word down. Spell it out loud as you write, keeping the picture of the word in your mind.

8   When you have written it, uncover the word and check to see if you are right.

Pause–prompt–praise

Pause–prompt–praise is an approach to helping children with their reading that encourages them to engage with the letters and words that they find difficult, and to use their word 'attack' skills. It is useful in many contexts when children are finding reading, and other skills, difficult.

When listening to a child read and they come to a word that they cannot manage, follow the route set out below:

1   Do not give the word straight away.

2   Pause.

3   If an attempt (or a guess) is not made, prompt. This means:
   ■ Ask what letter/sound the word begins with.
   ■ Ask the child to break the word up into syllables (e.g. Man-ches-ter).
   ■ Remind them to look for clues in any pictures.
   ■ Ask them to read forward or back to look for clues in the rest of the sentence.
   ■ If the word is obviously too difficult, tell them what it says and ask them to say it.
   ■ If they manage to work out what the word is, give praise; a simple 'good' or 'well done'.

Other points:

■ Try to make the experience enjoyable.

■ Take a positive view and avoid criticism.

■ Avoid allowing a child to struggle with reading material that is clearly too difficult.

■ Be sensitive about the child's feelings about reading aloud. Choose somewhere where they will not be overheard, especially if they are likely to find it difficult.

■ Praise good work, but do not over praise.

■ Be sure that the reading material is at an appropriate level of difficulty.

Useful contacts

Asperger's syndrome

See 'autism', below.

Attachment disorder

There is very little web-based support for this condition. The Attachment Disorder Research Trust is now owned by a care and education provider (Keys), which provides a range of specialist care, but not information or support of any other type. The Family Futures Consortium is an adoption support organisation that does have some information of relevance.

■ www.familyfutures.co.uk
■ www.keyschildcare.co.uk

Attention deficit disorder

ADDISS (Attention Deficit Disorder Information and Support Service) offers support for parents, sufferers and professionals.

■ www.addiss.co.uk

Autism

Research Autism is a UK charity dedicated to research into interventions in autism.

■ www.autismuk.com
■ www.researchautism.net

Cerebral palsy

Scope is a UK charity working to support and educate as well as fund research into cerebral palsy.

■ www.scope.org.uk

Conduct disorder

The Royal College of Psychiatrists offers a point of reference for support covering a range of psychological/psychiatric (and other) conditions.

■ www.rcpsych.ac.uk/expertadvice/youthinfo.aspx

Down's syndrome

The Down's Syndrome Association is a UK charity working for those with the syndrome.

■ www.downs-syndrome.org.uk

Dyslexia

British Dyslexia Association provides information for anyone with an interest in dyslexia. Their website talks and can change colour.

■ www.bdadyslexia.org.uk

Dyspraxia

The Dyspraxia Foundation provides support and information for individuals, families and professionals affected by dyspraxia.

■ www.dyspraxiafoundation.org.uk

Fragile X

The National Fragile X Foundation provides support, education and funds research into Fragile X.

■ www.fragilex.org

Obsessive–compulsive disorder

The Obsessive Compulsive Foundation is an international organisation dedicated to helping those with obsessive–compulsive disorder and related problems.

■ www.ocfoundation.org

Specific language impairment

These are UK charities supporting children and young people, their families and the professionals who work with them.

■ www.afasicengland.org.uk
■ www.thecommunicationtrust.org.uk
■ www.talkingpoint.org.uk/Teachers.aspx

Unusually, but perhaps appropriately for this area, or indeed for the more visual/auditory learners amongst our readers, this reference is to a video clip that, in turn, leads to a series of very helpful videos from the Raise Awareness of Language Learning Impairments (RALLI) campaign:

■ www.youtube.com/user/RALLIcampaign?feature=watch

Tourette's syndrome

Tourette's Action provides support, education and funds research into the condition.

■ www.tourettes-action.org.uk/

Williams syndrome

Provides information about the condition, and support and help to UK-based families dealing with the syndrome.

■ www.williams-syndrome.org.uk

7

The impact of neuroeducational research

There is probably no faster moving area of research related to education and learning than that of neuroscience and its links to psychology and learning. Gilbert (2008) tells us that it is argued that 95 per cent of what is known about the brain has been discovered in the last 15 years – which, if true, is remarkable. Since Gilbert wrote, the pace of increase in what is known about the brain – its structure, its functioning, its relationship to behaviour and learning – has, if anything, increased. Indeed, this area of research and scholarship now has a name of its own: 'neuroeducational research'. The rapid expansion of what is known about the physical structure of the brain, and the possibilities that this has for our deeper understanding of so many aspects of life, is a result of, first, the intense interest and industriousness of those involved in neuroscience, psychology and the practicalities of teaching and learning, and, second, the incredible technical developments that have taken place, and continue to take place, in the field of brain-scanning techniques. These two reasons feed one into the other. Vastly improved technical 'machinery' allowing us to look deeper, and with more clarity, into the working brain has given insights that have in themselves raised more questions and stimulated more detailed investigations. In turn, this has created demand for even more advanced techniques in the field of theoretical and applied physics, allowing for even more detailed examination of the minutiae of the brain at an incredibly high level of focus. The first magnetic resonance imaging (MRI) scan of an entire human body was undertaken in 1977. Techniques and technology have improved enormously since then, and, for some applications requiring finer and deeper levels of detail and accuracy, have been superseded by functional magnetic resonance imaging (fMRI). The workings and history of scanning techniques is fascinating, but this is not really the place to expand on it. One of the reasons for the massively increased research effort into neuroscience generally, and neuroeducational research in particular, is the commitment given to it by governments. The United States President Barack Obama has pledged US$3 billion (£1.96 billion) over ten years to an initiative called 'Brain Research through Advancing Innovative Neurotechnologies (BRAIN)'. The aim of BRAIN is to 'map the individual cells and circuits that make up the human brain, a project that will give scientists a better understanding of how a healthy brain works and how to devise better treatments for injuries and diseases of the brain' (Mason and Steenhuysen 2013). It is hoped – and, indeed, it is inevitable – that there will be big spin-offs for teaching and learning associated with this project. Similarly, in Europe, the European Commission granted €1 billion (£873 million) to a project that aims to create a model of the workings of the brain (Lee 2013, see also EC 2012). This underlines the high importance given to research in this area.

A great deal has been written about the brain and its role in learning over the years since the earlier editions of this book were published. Indeed, much has been written recently to challenge some of the points included in those earlier editions. Through re-writing this chapter, therefore, it is intended to look at what have become known as myths in this fast-developing field.

Neuroscience and neuro-myths

Howard-Jones considers that there is a 'parallel world of pseudo-neuroscience found in many schools' (2011). This parallel world is where much of the well-publicised – and, perhaps, over-hyped – advice based on the partially understood and sometimes ill-conceived knowledge about the brain is peddled.

Based on his earlier research (Howard-Jones *et al.* 2009), he lists a number of myths that seem to be held as truths by some in the world of education. He also identifies several other items from a list of so-called 'brain-based' truths, and shows that there may be evidence to support them. In doing so, he elucidates the 'parallel world of pseudo-neuroscience' noted earlier.

Howard-Jones is clear that there is no reliable evidence to support the following claims:

- Children are less attentive after sugary drinks and snacks.
- Environments that are rich in stimulus improve the brains of preschool children.
- Individuals learn better when they receive information in their preferred learning style (e.g. visual, auditory, kinaesthetic).
- Short bouts of co-ordination exercises can improve integration of left and right hemispheric brain function.
- Differences in hemispheric dominance (left brain, right brain) can help explain individual differences among learners.
- Learning problems associated with developmental differences in brain function cannot be remediated by education.

- Exercises that rehearse co-ordination of motor perception skills can improve literacy skill.
- Drinking less than six to eight glasses of water a day can cause the brain to shrink.

It is interesting to consider the background to some of the above. Several items from this list have featured heavily in the popular press, spurred on by many different forms of dissemination – courses and conferences, supposed learned texts, magazine and journal articles. Indeed, there is quite a collection of anecdotal evidence that is presented in support of many of the ideas. It is, as we have seen, largely unsupported by rigorous scientific investigation or validated by peer review, but, despite this, many teachers have applied what they have been told, and believe that, by applying, for example, the practice of regular physical activity prior to classroom-based work that needs concentration and application, their pupils work better and produce work of higher than usual quality. This they may then ascribe to better-integrated brain hemispheres. It may well be the case that the class works better, but there is no real evidence to show that this has anything to do with stimulating the brain into better operation in the way that has been suggested. Indeed, there may well be any number of explanations for the noted improvements in 'output'. Not least of these might be teacher expectation, to suggest but one. The psychology of the dynamics of the classroom is a complex area, and it is known that teacher, or even pupil, expectation can play a very important role in what actually happens. If a class of children is told that drinking water at regular intervals will improve their ability to concentrate, with the associated improvements in their work, then it is possible that this will indeed come to pass. Thirsty children are likely to be restless, and, for that reason, not work well in class. Any perceived improvement in children's work and attainment as a result of free access to water can be explained in different ways. For this reason, it is very important that educational innovations are carefully and scientifically tested before they are absorbed into usual practice.

Howard-Jones, at the same time as exposing some of the current neuro–myths, tells us that there is evidence to support the following statements:

- Regular drinking of caffeinated soft drinks reduces alertness.
- There are no critical periods in childhood after which you cannot learn some things, just sensitive periods when it is easier.
- Vigorous exercise can improve mental function.
- Individual learners show preferences for the mode in which they receive information (e.g. visual, auditory, kinaesthetic).
- Production of new connections in the brain can continue into old age.
- Extended rehearsal of some mental processes can change the shape and structure of some parts of the brain.

Brain plasticity

When Minsky wrote that 'The principal activities of brains are making changes in themselves' (1986), he was actually striking at the very centre of what is so vitally important about the brain and about learning, although he was founding his ideas on a greatly reduced research base compared with what is known now. Moreover, he was referring to the notion of brain plasticity, which is also something about which so much more is now known.

Learning, as we know, is the process by which new knowledge, concepts and skills are acquired though experience, including instruction or teaching, and memory is the mechanism by which knowledge and other new learning is retained over time. We refer to the brain's capacity to change as learning progresses as 'plasticity'. Drubach (2000) suggests two types of observable modifications to the brain as learning takes place:

1 A change in the internal structure of the neurons, the most notable being in the area of synapses.
2 An increase in the number of synapses between neurons.

In the same way that we considered schemas (Chapter 3) to be almost infinitely variable between individuals who know, or who have learnt, the same things, the brain exhibits massive variability for making and re-making connections between nerve cells. The brain is made up of more than 100 billion separate cells, or neurones. The important point about 'intelligence' and the lowly neurone is not to do with how many an individual might have, but with the number of connections that have been made between them. In answer to the question, 'Did Einstein have a very large brain?', the answer is, 'No, his brain was smaller than average, because he was a smaller-than-average man. His intelligence came from the number of connections he had between his brain cells.' Every time learning takes place, new connections are made between two or more neurones. The brain is, in a sense, moulded by our experiences of everyday life in general and by specific learning situations. Every time learning takes place, new links are made, and every time the same learning is used or rehearsed, the links become stronger and, in doing so, become more fixed. The patterns of links between neurones are referred to as templates, and each individual item of learning has its own precise template. We have billions of templates and many more billions of individual links between cells. The more we learn, the greater the number of links that are made and the more complex the already complex patterns of connection become.

The younger we are, the greater is this plasticity effect. This means that the young have a great potential for learning – but it does not mean that older dogs cannot learn new tricks! It seems that new learning is always possible. As long as new experience comes along, and the will to engage with new ideas and skills exists, the plasticity of the brain will continue.

Two hemispheres

Even though much of what has historically been believed about the two hemi-spheres of the brain has been shown to be incorrect in the light of recent research, it is of interest to briefly review some of this 'past knowledge' in order to consider some of the approaches that have been advocated in the more recent past.

As recently as 1997 (since when, a great deal of work has been carried out and a great deal of new understanding established), it was written that: 'The left brain specialises in academic aspects of learning – language and mathematical pro-cesses, logical thoughts, sequences and analysis. The right brain is principally concerned with creative activities utilising rhyme, rhythm, music, visual impres-sions, colour and pictures' (Rose and Nicholl 1997). Put simply, by this view, one hemisphere is predominantly concerned with the logical and the other with the more creative. We now know that this is not the case.

It was thought that one or other of the hemispheres was dominant in certain activities, but now it is known that both are involved in almost all of our thinking. It was thought that those of us who are 'left brained' tend to favour a slow, step-by-step build up of information and learning proceeds in a linear fashion, while those of us who are 'right brained' prefer to see the whole picture, to have an overview, and learning is a more global or holistic activity. This view has affected, and continues to influence, many in the education system.

It is a physiological fact that the brain is made up of two large hemispheres that are joined centrally. The right-side hemisphere controls the motor move-ment of the left side of the body, and the right side of the body is controlled by the left hemisphere. As for the more intellectual functions of the two hemi-spheres, it is important not to stress, or even consider, the different functions of the hemispheres because the almost infinite complexity of the brain works holis-tically, with both hemispheres engaged to lesser and greater degrees in all of our mental activity.

More recent research has led to a description of the two hemispheres of the brain, and their functions and relationship to each other, rather differently. One way of describing brain hemispheric function and speciality is that the brain does have two separate hemispheres, which operate both independently and in tandem, and which appear to operate differently from each other (Curran and Gilbert 2008). It seems that the split between hemispheres – previously consid-ered as a dichotomy between linear and logical and creative and holistic – is now perceived more along the lines of an intellectual versus emotional divide. The right hemisphere is deemed to work in an emotionally biased way, and the left in a more intellectual way. However, some doubt is placed on this notion by current researchers.

We will see later that emotion, and the emotional structure of the mid brain or limbic system, is an incredibly important evolutionary change in human brains that sets them apart from the majority of the animal kingdom in terms of thought and action, and allows for a vast degree of conscious thought.

Parts of each hemisphere are mirrored in the other and some functions are shared. Sometimes – in the case of language, for example – there are matched areas in both sides of the brain, but their functions are slightly different. This has been described as 'complementary hemispheric specialisation' (Heilman and Gilmore 1998), and renders the rigid differentiation that is sometimes put forward far less convincing. There are certain areas of the brain, however, that have specialist functions – in language, for example – and damage to this area can lead to a loss of certain aspects of language, but other aspects may well be unaffected.

Having said all of this, we should be asking what impact this knowledge can have on learning activities in the classroom. The answer might well be 'very little', although the rate of growth of new discoveries about the structure and function of the brain is rapid, and new findings might well have an impact on teaching and, therefore, learning in the future. The point remains that precise location of intellectual or emotional centres of the brain does not affect what teachers plan and do. However, an understanding that these different 'systems' are present is very important. We will see, in the next section, that emotion and appealing to emotion in learning situations can have a big influence on learning and on its longevity.

The triune brain

The neuroscientist Paul MacLean expanded on the theory of the 'triune brain' (1974; 1989), which complements the description of the two hemispheres and their respective functions. Largely, MacLean's work has been superseded by newer findings in the realm of neuroscience. Nonetheless, we will consider it here, though only in brief, since it sheds light on some aspects of human behaviour and, in a limited way, can help in the understanding of such things as emotional responses to a variety of situations. If not strictly supported by science, the descriptions and explanations given in this theory are helpful in a 'day-to-day' way.

The triune brain ('triune' meaning a trinity or three in one) was first identified in the 1950s, and has been expanded upon in later work (e.g. MacLean 1974; 1989). The notion of the triune brain offers a simplified model of the way that the brain functions. It should go without saying that the brain is a highly complex organ, having more than 100 billion active nerve cells, each of which is capable of producing 20,000 to 50,000 branches. There are approximately another 900 billion cells that support and protect the nerve cells. The brain functions in a far more complex way than we currently understand, and MacLean's model does not purport to do more than illustrate some key elements of the way that the brain operates. The three elements of the structure of the brain, according to MacLean, are:

1   *The reptilian or instinctive brain.* The reptilian brain controls muscles, balance and autonomic functions (such as breathing and heartbeat) and is always active, even when we are in deep sleep. This part of the brain has the same type of simplistic and instinctive behavioural programmes as snakes and

lizards, which is where its name comes from. When someone is placed under stress, the reptilian brain takes over. A learner does not respond when the instinctive brain is in control, because this part of the brain operates in basic, ritualistic responses, such as flight or fight. We will consider the importance of this aspect of the brain's function in learning situations later.

2   *The mid-brain or emotional brain* (also known as the 'limbic system'). The role of this part of the brain is to control emotions, and it is thought to be the location of the long-term memory. Sometimes referred to as the 'mammalian brain', this part of the brain corresponds to the brain of most mammals. The mammalian brain is concerned with emotions and instincts, feeding, fighting, fleeing and sexual behaviour, all at a higher level than the instinctive brain. The mid-brain controls such things as the immune system, eating patterns and sleeping cycles. When there is an emotional connection with learning, the mid-brain is engaged and involved. When something connected to a learning experience is funny, sad or exciting, the memory of the event and the likelihood of the learning becoming lasting and meaningful are greatly increased.

3   *The neo-cortex*, which is divided into the right and left hemispheres. It is also known as the 'superior' or 'rational' (neo-mammalian) brain. The neo-cortex is close in structure to the brains of the primate mammals. The higher cognitive functions that distinguish humans from the other animals are in the neo-cortex. In humans, the neo-cortex takes up two-thirds of the total brain mass. The two hemispheres are joined by the corpus callosum, which carries messages between the two sides. This part of the brain is involved in problem solving, discerning relationships and patterns of meaning. The neo-cortex will only function if the other parts of the brain allow it to. For this reason, a calm and composed environment is essential for learning and, in particular, for advanced, abstract and creative thought.

The reptilian brain is simple and, in many cases, functions on a limited number of actions, which are set and unchangeable. The most advanced lizards still only have a reptilian brain, and rely for their safety, well being and reproduction on a relatively small repertoire of actions (27, we are told by Curran (2008)). These actions include simple algorithms for moving from a hot place to a cooler one, moving from a cool place to a warmer one, taking a submissive posture when confronted by a bigger lizard, but an aggressive posture when coming across a smaller relative.

It is the emotional functions, possibly located in the limbic brain, that have crucial importance for learning. We appear to learn more effectively when the content of the learning is associated with emotion. Emotions ranging from extreme fear to overbearing pleasure and all points between can have bearing in learning situations. For our purposes, we will limit ourselves to thinking about school learning situations. If every learning situation is bland and uninteresting, there is little chance that any sense of fun or enjoyment will be generated. Conversely, if activities are made to be enjoyable or exciting, or even slightly risky (in some safe way), emotions are likely to be engaged and the connections made in the brain that lead to effective, lasting learning are likely to be stronger and more durable. This notion is borne out, anecdotally, by practitioners.

The idea that pupils should be in fear of their teacher is worthy of mention here. The use of sheer terror as a teaching strategy is not to be recommended, although the prospect of severe punishment has been used in the past. Fear is an emotion that may well engender some forms of effective learning – fear of being cut by a sharp knife, for example – but, as we will see later, the negative stress that situations of fear can generate is not good for learning. It is, at a simple level, the low-level emotions brought about by positive relationships between teacher and learner that can have the most immediate impact on a learner's success. If the child likes the teacher (and vice versa), learning can often progress smoothly. This is obviously very difficult to legislate for, but we should be aware that positive and constructive, rather than any sort of destructive, relationships in learning situations should be sought. In challenging classroom conditions, this can be extremely difficult – and, even in calmer situations, time is required to build relationships. None of this is to suggest that teachers should attempt to befriend and become bosom pals with the children in their class. Many trainee teachers make this mistake, and then pay the price when issues of control arise, but positive and evolving relationships that maintain certain boundaries are likely to lead to effective and emotionally satisfying learning.

We will now look in turn at some of the main points raised by a new and growing awareness of the role of the brain in learning. We will also consider the views of some of the movement's detractors.

Principles of brain-based learning

There is a list of 12 principles (Caine and Caine 1997) that, it is said, apply to learning, and which can be located in the sphere of the brain and of neuroeducational research generally; we will look at these principles briefly below. (Interestingly, the writers of these principles have been accused, albeit indirectly, of propagating the myths associated with what became known as 'brain-based learning'; see above.) The principles are not final and they should be viewed as evolving (Caine and Caine 1997). It will be clear to readers of more recent and more rigorously monitored research that the science underpinning these principles is not sound. However, they are worthy of consideration because they have a resonance with practitioners, who have found that some of them have led to learning improvements when put into practice. The principles are:

1 The brain is a complex adaptive system.
2 The brain is a social brain.
3 The search for meaning is innate.
4 The search for meaning occurs through patterning.
5 Emotions are critical to patterning.

6 Every brain simultaneously perceives and creates parts and wholes.

7 Learning involves both focused attention and peripheral attention.

8 Learning always involves conscious and unconscious processes.

9 We have at least two ways of organising memory.

10 Learning is developmental.

11 Complex learning is enhanced by challenge and inhibited by threat.

12 Every brain is uniquely organised.

The brain is a complex adaptive system

The brain can function simultaneously on many levels and in many different ways. The brain is continuously monitoring and processing thoughts, emotions, imagination and predispositions, operating at a physiological level. There is also a neurophysiological system, which interacts with and exchanges information with its environment and works in parallel with and in conjunction with the other elements that make up the brain. A great many brain functions are hidden from our consciousness – controlling our breathing, for example, and a very large number of other essential activities. As the process of learning is complex and multifaceted, learning can – and should – be approached in a variety of different ways. This idea has certain resonances with what we know about learning styles, and about the importance of the context of learning and the need for learning to be more than mundane.

An example of this idea of variety is that based on the V–A–K description of learning styles by Levine (2003). He recommends transforming a verbal into a visual task, and a visual task into a kinaesthetic task. In this way, he suggests, a certain challenge is presented to the brain, not a continuous flow of the same approaches. The notion of 'activity shifting' and teaching to accommodate a range of learning preferences is also considered to be important. Many teachers, in fact, do not need to be told this; changing activity or approach to the same content is an approach advocated by many educators and followed by many teachers. A 'contrasting activity' is often a feature in many lessons. The reason why a contrasting activity is used to good effect can be related to a variety of theoretical underpinnings, not least the need for challenge and variety.

The brain is a social brain

The brain responds to social engagement. Work with others can be a stimulus to greater enjoyment of learning and to deeper levels of thought about the topic in question. The notion of the social brain, though not couched in identical terms, can be seen to form a part of the movement towards collaborative learning and working in groups, which has developed out of the work of the social constructivists, including Vygotsky and Bruner, who both stress the importance of dialogue and the use of language as a medium for learning. Learning is deeply influenced by social interactions and relationships.

The search for meaning is innate

Humans strive to make sense of what they experience, and this can, perhaps, be described as the human brain functioning effectively. Humans instinctively want to know that learning has purpose and value. In part, this is a survival instinct. An understanding of the seasons, for example, or the habits of small edible creatures can mean the difference between survival and death. For some, this involves a search for meaning in the very nature of creation; for others, at a more immediate level, the need to know why they are asked to complete a particular task in a particular lesson becomes important, and this question should be answered. When teachers share with the class the purpose of what they are doing – the learning objectives, not just what they have to do – then the need for under-standing and meaning can, in part, be satisfied.

The search for meaning occurs through patterning

When new ideas are encountered, we make great efforts to link them with prior knowledge and experience that is in some way related to them. This complies with the description of human memory put forward by cognitive constructivist psychologists. Schema theory suggests that new information is linked to and associated with other similar information. If it is difficult to retrieve previously encountered knowledge or experience, then learning the new content does not proceed smoothly. Prior knowledge – and, in particular, the activation of this prior knowledge – is very important in new learning. The links and new associations form ever more complex patterns of knowledge and understanding, and it seems that drawing the learner's attention to the structures of their existing schemas and using them to integrate new information facilitates the process of pattern building and leads to more effective learning. The activation of prior knowledge is seen as an essential step preceding the introduction of new material and opening up a sound foundation for new learning.

The brain seems to have the ability to resist the 'imposition of meaningless-ness'. By 'meaninglessness', Caine and Caine (1997) mean isolated pieces of information unrelated to what makes sense to a particular learner. They continue by saying that effective education must give learners opportunities to generate their own patterns of understanding.

Emotions are critical to patterning

'Emotional intelligence' was first described by Salovey and Mayer (1990), and further developed by Goleman (1998). Goleman describes emotional intelli-gence as 'the capacity for recognizing our own feelings, and those of others, for motivating ourselves and for managing emotions well in ourselves and in our relationships'. Emotional intelligence describes abilities that are distinct from, but work alongside, what can be called 'academic intelligence'.

If an individual is in a state of emotional unrest, for whatever reason, it is likely that he or she will not be able to function effectively as a learner. Obviously, a sensitive teacher will take account of the emotional climate in a classroom, but, more importantly, a teacher should ensure that the nature of the classroom and the nature of teaching approaches should not lead to emotional unrest in a class or in an individual. We will consider this further when we review the idea of 'relaxed alertness', below.

Every brain simultaneously perceives and creates parts and wholes

Left/right brain research is only the beginning of understanding the way the brain divides learning tasks between verbal and visual, analytical and global, logical and creative. Successful teachers engage learners in tasks that require both sides of the brain to engage. An example of this might be using art in maths lessons, or music to help the understanding of a scientific principle. In some classrooms, cross-disciplinary approaches are taken that attempt to embrace the different facets of the brain's structure and function. According to the political climate, this notion of an integrated approach to learning is either promoted or discouraged. In any case, it can be seen as an attempt to, among other things, recognise and work with the interaction of both left and right hemispheres.

Learning involves both focused attention and peripheral attention

The brain takes in information directly, but is also able to give attention to what have been called 'fringe thoughts' (Ruggiero 2000). These fringe thoughts, referred to as 'peripheral signals' by Caine and Caine (1997), can be very potent and can even obscure what should be the main focus of the teaching. We are capable of both paying attention to the main point of reference in a teaching situation and, at the same time, being aware of many of the peripheral or background events that may be present. This has implications for the classroom environment, since, sometimes, the peripheral events can take over from the main event in terms of holding a learner's attention. It also has implications for hidden messages transmitted, sometimes inadvertently, by teachers (via the medium of body language, for example).

Learning always involves conscious and unconscious processes

At a surface level, it is fairly easy to assess what facts may have been learnt or what new information has been retained. It is far more difficult to assess the depth of understanding that may have developed during the completion of a learning task. There is an enormous amount of unconscious processing taking place in our brains, not just at times of learning, but almost all of the time, and more so when there is a conscious effort being made and conscious mental activity is being undertaken. The creation of connections between ideas and growth in conceptual understanding can take time. Often, time for reflection is needed to allow for ideas to 'sink in'. This reflection time is a time when ideas can be revisited and reconsidered. Reflection on newly covered work is a time when, sometimes with encouragement, connections can be made and some of the important unconscious processing can be brought to the surface.

We have at least two ways of organising memory

Differing theories concerning the structure and form of long- and short-term memory have been with us for many years. Caine and Caine (1994) refer to O'Keefe and Nadel's (1978) model and explain the two types of memory as 'taxon/locale' and 'spatial/autobiographical'. Taxon/locale memory is motivated by rewards and punishments. Recall is not related directly to specific links, and often unrelated information can be accessed in what might appear to be a random fashion. Spatial/autobiographical memory is much more related to the links and associations between events, particularly when personal experience is involved. In this type of learning, recall can be instant and is more reliant on the logic of links formed at the time of the event in question.

These two types of memory help learners to record their experiences, as important and unimportant details are categorised and stored differently. Teachers can attend to both types of memory by organising activities into meaningful parts, placing ideas in context and incorporating a range of learning styles and multiple intelligences into classroom practice.

Learning is developmental

Work in the 1980s by Diamond *et al.* (1986) gave insight into the way that the brain is able to grow and produce more physical connections than had previously been thought possible. It had been thought that the brain's structure was fixed early in the developmental process and that the growth of new physical pathways was not a real possibility. They describe this ability to grow expansive networks of nervous pathways and connections as 'dendritic fireworks'. This refers to the idea that dendrites – the physical but microscopic branches of nerves in the brain that control the movement of electrical nervous impulses – have the ability to grow incredibly rapidly and in many different directions, creating new and complex patterns of neural connections.

Complex learning is enhanced by challenge and inhibited by threat

For many teachers, the notion of differentiation – pitching work at an appropriate level of difficulty for an individual – has become an important element of their work. This has not been done for 'brain-based' reasons. We have come to see, based on the work of Piaget and Vygotsky, that learning will not proceed if the material offered is either too complex or too simple. There is a 'brain-based' explanation, however. If teaching is pitched too low, the brain-based community tells us that the learners will be under-stimulated. If teaching is at the precise level of the learner, they work in what has been called a 'comfort zone', where little new learning will take place. Teaching at a slightly elevated level, where challenge is provided but the work is not impossible, encourages our learners to engage with the work. This is a very accurate reflection of the work of Vygotsky and the zone of proximal development.

The notion of 'threat' has links to the emotional state of the learner. It is fairly well known that, when in a state of stress, induced perhaps by perceived threats of one sort or another, we fail to function effectively. The idea of fight or flight comes into play, and it is very unlikely that a child will be able to work at even the simplest level of difficulty in a situation where they are experiencing any sort of negative stress.

Every brain is uniquely organised

We have seen earlier that individuals differ from one another in a number of ways. This can, in part, be explained by the different experiences that we have, but it is also partly related to the structure and make-up of an individual's brain. We have also seen that, in virtually identical learning situations, different patterns of connections might be made by different individuals and different, but similar, templates will be formed. Again, this relates directly to the formation of schemas and the fact that new learning depends upon what is already known. Levine (2002) described a 'myth of laziness', referring to the perception that a teacher, or other adult, may form of a child based on observed problems with a child's attitude in teaching situations. He suggests that the attitudinal problems, which can result in a number of unhelpful behaviour patterns in the classroom, may stem from a variety of unaddressed problems. Some of the problems may be a result of the unique organisation of the learner's brain. This can be seen to refer to multiple intelligence theory, or to notions of cognitive and learning preference. It is possible that some learners, given the right kind of support in organising their learning through tailored work plans or alternative approaches, can improve their attitudes and behaviour and show marked improvement in their schoolwork. If a small amount of success can be achieved, this can lead to further success and to the well-known benefits associated with succeeding.

Caine and Caine (1997) conclude by saying that: 'Optimizing the use of the human brain means using the brain's infinite capacity to make connections, and understanding what conditions maximize this process.' They identify three 'interactive and mutually supportive' elements that should be present in order for complex learning to take place:

1 an optimal state of mind that we call *relaxed alertness*, consisting of low threat and high challenge;

2 the *orchestrated immersion* of the learner in multiple, complex, authentic experiences;

3 the regular, *active processing* of experience as the basis for making meaning.

We will look at each of these in turn.

Relaxed alertness

If it is true that '80 per cent of learning difficulties are related to stress' (Stokes and Whiteside 1984), then it should be seen as an absolute priority for teachers to ensure that the learning environment for which they have responsibility is as free of stress as possible. It is the state of relaxed alertness that, in ideal situations, would ensure a stress-free working environment.

Renate Caine advises that 'if children are to think critically, they must feel safe to take risks' (Poole 1997). It is generally agreed that teachers should strive to create a 'safe' learning environment for learning to proceed effectively. The requirements for teachers in training in England and Wales (TDA 2007) give a comprehensive and detailed set of standards, all of which must be met, including several that relate to the teaching environment. Teachers are expected to be able to demonstrate that they have high expectations of children and young people and a commitment to ensuring that they can achieve their full educational potential. We all know, from our own personal experience, that our ability to think coherently can be compromised in situations of even limited stress – job interviews and consultations with medical professionals are two examples of this. This is the case in classrooms when, for whatever reason, children experience negative stress. Some writers emphasise the negative aspects of stress, while others highlight the fact that a little stress is likely to enhance performance. Ellis (1973) describes three varieties of stress: negative stress, distress and positive stress, which he calls 'eustress'. Eustress is sometimes referred to as pleasant, or curative, stress. Positive stress, in small doses, can be used in a constructive way; it can lead to heightened performance and alter attitudes and behaviour. It can also have a positive effect on self-esteem. However, the damaging effects of excessive negative stress are to be avoided and the brain-based school of thought considers that stress is, in general terms, counterproductive in terms of effective learning.

Orchestrated immersion

'Orchestrated immersion' refers to a situation in which children can become fully involved in the topic in question. There are various suggestions about how this might be achieved, but, in general terms, topics need to be made interesting and accessible. The idea of orchestrated immersion is clearly related to the notions of context and engagement that were discussed in earlier chapters. It is important that the immersion should be orchestrated – meaning well structured and developmental, and in the control of the teacher.

Active processing

Active processing is an important principle, and, again, is related to ideas discussed earlier. As we will see, some of the detractors of brain-based theory comment on the closeness of brain-based precepts to elements of what is known and described in other theoretical frameworks. In the case of active processing, the importance of what the constructivists call 'mental processing' and the emphasis laid on engagement and understanding are clearly very close to each other.

Active processing includes relating what is new to previous experiences and to real-life events. This, too, is related very closely to the constructivist notion of all new learning being built upon a foundation of what has gone before, and the importance, in practical terms, of relating new to old and 'activating prior knowledge' in order to ease the process of new learning.

Orchestrated immersion and active processing should work together to assist learners in seeing a wider perspective than is sometimes offered in lessons. The ability to connect specific elements of teaching and learning with 'the big picture' is an important part of the brain-based approach.

Situated learning, authentic contexts, the importance of prior learning and engagement – all important in the context of constructivist learning theory – all feature, though in a slightly different guise, in the vocabulary and toolbox of the advocates of the brain-based approach. Also under the broad umbrella of the brain-based perspective, but from a physiological standpoint, there are other important considerations. For the brain to function effectively, there are three important physical prerequisites. These are:

1 the brain's need for an adequate supply of oxygen;
2 the brain's need for an adequate supply of water;
3 the brain's need for adequate nutrition.

The brain also has a need for rest, and so the need for sleep in young learners is shown to be very important. All teachers recognise that sleep-deficient children do not make effective learners.

Concentration span

The length of time that a learner can concentrate is a crucial aspect of how learning can be structured. In particular, the length of time for which teachers expect their pupils to listen to them can be critical. It is said (though it is very difficult to find research-based evidence for this) that a child's concentration span, in minutes, is equal to the age of the child plus two. It is also said (again, without any sort of referenced evidence) that a child's concentration span, in minutes, is the child's age less one. In either case, this is not very long. The average concentration of an American adult is thought to be seven minutes, which purportedly accounts for the time between adverts in American television programmes, while the British adult concentration span is supposed to be slightly longer, at 11 minutes; however, elsewhere it is suggested that the 'average adult' has a concentration span of 20 minutes. All of the easily traceable reports on concentration span seem to neglect to cite their sources.

Irrespective of this, the observation that children seem to have very short concentration spans is of importance to teachers. Long introductory phases to lessons will fall on deaf ears after the few minutes of concentration have elapsed.

Detractors

We have looked at Howard-Jones' 'myths' above, but we should also consider what was written 15 years earlier, when the first notions of brain-based learning were being commercially promoted to teachers. Bruer (1997), in his article 'Education and the brain: a bridge too far', gives a very early, comprehensive and rigorously supported argument against the claims made by some of so-called 'brain-based learning' advocates, showing that we would all be wise to treat several of the claims with great caution. He says of some of the ideas central to brain-based theory: 'These ideas have been around for a decade, are often based on misconceptions and overgeneralizations of what we know about the brain, and have little to offer to educators' (Bruer 1997). He examined 'a set of claims that I will call the "neuroscience and education argument". The negative conclusion is that the argument fails. The argument fails because its advocates are trying to build a bridge too far' (Bruer 1997).

Bruer is not alone in his concern over the claims made for brain-based learning. Ravitch (2000) considers brain-based learning a troubling trend and a 'distortion of what cognitive scientists have learnt about how children learn'. She suggests that brain-based learning might be a commercial bandwagon, and that the proliferation of companies offering expensive workshops and related resources are evidence of this.

Jensen's worldwide bestseller *Teaching with the Brain in Mind* (1998; cited in Killion 1999; 2002), in many ways seen as the leading text of the brain-based approach to teaching, has been heavily criticised for its style-over-content approach, for its lack of scientific rigour and for being an ideas book rather than a research-based factual account.

Despite having some detractors (even such reputable detractors as Bruer), many established educators and researchers give credence to the theory and practice encompassed within the broad scope of the brain-based learning movement. Many teachers who have engaged with only small elements of the breadth of what is included in brain-based learning are reasonably well enough convinced that it makes a positive difference to learning that they choose to

continue and to develop its use. Many teachers, for example, advocate the implementation of such ideas as the provision of water, intermittent physical activity,
an insight into the 'big picture' and the sharing of learning objectives. Numerous
teachers would agree that a relaxed atmosphere is likely to lead to better learning
outcomes, and strive to achieve such an environment for their classrooms. There
are schools where new approaches to much of the delivery of the curriculum are
being implemented based upon some of the brain-based learning principles
described here. Time will be the judge of the real efficacy of the approaches, and
we must watch carefully to ensure that opportunities for making real headway
with teaching and learning are not lost. The neuroscientists themselves are clear
that there will be more from their domain in the future. Susan Greenfield, an
eminent and well-known researcher of the brain, writing in *The Times Educational
Supplement* (2005), said that:

> Brain research is poised, if it can rise to the challenge, to make the biggest
> contribution of all to how the brain learns through interaction with the
> environment. [. . .] Now, more than ever before, educationalists and brain
> scientists need to work together.

Certainly, these words seem to have been fulfilled – though, perhaps, not
fully fulfilled yet. Research into the brain, linked to education and learning, is
certainly moving on very quickly, and seems poised to go much further. For
teachers, it seems to be a case of 'watch this space' very closely.

Summary

Thanks to detailed brain research, largely undertaken by neuroscientists and
related to teaching by psychologists and other interested parties, we have at our
disposal a good deal of information about how the brain functions. Fun, excitement and positive relationships are almost prerequisite for learning to reach its
full potential. Teachers are not charged with turning every classroom event into
a comedy show, but laughter and real enjoyment do lead to starting points for
learning with great possibilities for effective learning. The brain does need food,
water and oxygen in order to function physiologically; hungry, thirsty learners
cannot be fully effective learners. The brain, or the learner, appears to need a
certain amount of challenge, but cannot function effectively under conditions of
negative stress. Learners seem to thrive in conditions where activity is encouraged and patterns are allowed to develop. Learning in broad contexts with
connections to other areas of understanding seems to be beneficial. Classrooms
that provide a safe and stimulating environment, allowing for what are known as
'relaxed alertness', 'active processing' and 'orchestrated immersion', are likely to
lead to conditions for effective learning. Obviously, these conditions should exist
in conjunction with other conditions for learning, which are considered in the
other chapters of this book.

In the classroom

- Work hard to promote positive relationships.

- Attempt to inject teaching situations and tasks that are set with emotion-raising devices to promote enjoyment and excitement.

- Allow opportunities to drink water.

- Allow opportunities for movement. Even walking to collect a book from the front of the room is movement. Some determined efforts to encourage increased blood flow are perhaps better than leaving it to chance.

- Do not expect learners to concentrate beyond the limit of their concentration span. Break up activities with short contrasting sections to lessons, and have what is known as a 'new beginning'.

- Try to give insight into the 'bigger picture' and draw attention to patterns in and between different areas of the curriculum.

- Work towards a learning environment where there is:
  - relaxed alertness;
  - orchestrated immersion;
  - active processing.

As we have seen, the area of research covered in this chapter is fast moving and there is little doubt that the sum total of our understanding is set to increase greatly. For those of us with a specific interest in the implications of both current and further insights and developments, it is fairly clear that we should keep our eyes and ears wide open and ready to receive, analyse and, quite possibly, implement what are likely to be new, interesting and potentially very important developments as neuroeducational research strides forward.

8

Relating theory to practice

What can we learn from research?

> Schools exist to promote learning. Teachers are catalysts for learning.
>
> (Cohen *et al.* 2004)

Since the crucial role of catalyst for learning falls to teachers, it is very important that they have a detailed knowledge and awareness of the ways in which learning can be promoted in schools. This means that teachers need to know about what is currently considered as most important in terms of learning theory and the ways in which the theory can be translated into practice. If we look back at the preceding chapters, we can see that, in a teacher's bank of knowledge and understanding about learning, there is a place for behaviourism, cognitive and constructivist theory, including situated learning, metacognition, and social constructivism; for an understanding of learning styles and multiple intelligence theory; and for a knowledge of what the neuropsychologists/neuroeducationalists and others are discovering about effective learning contexts. As well as knowing about these areas of theory, teachers must be able to interpret and then apply to practice what it is that they know. A sound working knowledge of the major and common conditions that adversely affect the progress of learning is also important. In this final chapter, we will summarise and review the major components of what has been covered in the earlier chapters, and attempt to establish ways of working and organising for learning that will help teachers to provide contexts and activities that will prove to be effective and lead to the promotion of effective – and enjoyable – learning.

Wray and Lewis (1997) single out four aspects of learning that they consider to be of paramount importance. They are:

1 Learning is a process of interaction between what is known and what is to be learnt.

2 Learning is a social process.

3 Learning is situated.

4 Learning is a metacognitive process.

We can add that:

5 Learning can sometimes proceed in a rote fashion, with less understanding involved initially.

6 Learning can sometimes depend on an individual's preferred learning style.

7 Learning can be affected by certain conditions concerning the brain.

Let us now look at each of the seven points above, and consider more precisely what is meant by each of them and how practice might be affected by them.

Learning is a process of interaction between what is known and what is to be learnt

What is known (prior knowledge or pre-existing knowledge) is the knowledge, skill or ability that a learner brings to a new learning encounter. This includes all knowledge that is available before the learning event, and which has been gathered or developed by any means, and in any situation, including both formal and, quite often, informal learning situations. Learners need enough previous knowledge and understanding to enable them to learn new things; they also need help making links with new and previous knowledge explicit.

It is considered to be valuable to go through a process of what has been called 'activating prior knowledge'. Teachers often go through this process at the beginning of a new topic. They also use introductory strategies at the beginning of lessons that are continuations from previous lessons. In terms of the practicalities of teaching, this is a process of making children think about the topic or remember what has been covered already. In terms of theory, it is to do with activating particular schemas.

Teachers approach the activation of prior knowledge in a number of different ways. The effective approaches involve what is sometimes referred to as 'elicitation'. This is the process of drawing out from children what they already know, even if they do not realise that they know it. By careful questioning, a teacher can draw out from individual children, or even large groups of children, ideas, facts and notions that can be of direct relevance to the topic that the teacher wishes to introduce and develop.

Other strategies include asking children to bring to mind anything related to a topic. This approach has a number of different names, each having a slightly different shade of meaning: 'thought trawl'; 'mind shower'; 'ideas meet'; and also 'brainstorm', now considered inappropriate by some because of its medical associations. Children are asked simply to express ideas, facts or thoughts relating to an idea – 'heat', for example, or 'holidays' – or perhaps other possibly less abstract notions, such as 'pets'; people, too, can be used to good effect – 'King Henry

VIII', for example. Sometimes, a list is created; sometimes, each offering is discussed. Sometimes, the ideas are classified in some way or added to a chart. There are likely to be as many ways of dealing with an activity like this as there are teachers – and all are likely to be equally valid. They all serve the same purpose, which is to bring to the forefront of the mind of the individual child, or even to what could be considered a notional group consciousness, what it is that is known about a topic that is about to be introduced and developed through further teaching.

For a teacher, the process of activating the prior knowledge of the class is an important exploratory activity. The ideas, facts and thoughts presented by the class can give an important insight, not only into what is known, but also into possible misconceptions that may exist. This is valuable for teachers when deciding precisely which level or, more often, levels of difficulty to plan for, or in helping them to ascertain areas of the topic that seem to be well established and those that are not.

One useful tool available to teachers is known as a K–W–L grid. The acronym 'K–W–L' comes from: 'What do I *know*? What do I *want* to find out? What have I *learnt*?' The layout of the grid is largely immaterial. Teachers can provide a framework for children to write in, but this is not always necessary. The activation of prior knowledge element of the grid is the 'K'. Children are asked – and this could be individually, in pairs or in small groups – to write down what they know about a subject. The use of a K–W–L grid will assist the process of activating prior knowledge; with practice, children can develop their own, more sophisticated responses to this approach.

The next two elements of the grid are used subsequently, being a means of focusing attention onto specific questions to investigate and then noting the answers to questions formulated. Table 8.1 is an example of a completed K–W–L grid.

TABLE 8.1 K–W–L grid: animals in cold parts of the world

What do I already know?	What do I want to find out?	What have I learnt?
1 Polar bears, penguins and walruses live in the very cold parts of the world. 2 Penguins can't fly. 3 Emperor penguins are the biggest penguins.	1 What other animals live there? 2 Do they all fight or do they get on with each other? 3 Are there different sorts of polar bears? 4 Can they all swim?	1 Sea lions and seals, and different sorts of birds live there, too. 2 Penguins only live at the south pole and polar bears only live at the north pole and so they never meet. 3 There is only one main type of polar bear. There are lots of different penguins. 4 Polar bears are good swimmers.

The use of such a grid, or a similar approach, can encourage children to focus on what they already know about a topic. It can also allow them to identify what they would like to know about it, and then to plan and find something out and note what they have learnt. The K–W–L grid (alternatively known as 'prior knowledge and reaction') was first put forward by Ogle (1989) and has been further extended by Wray and Lewis (1997). It is an example of a device that can be used to good effect when helping children to activate their prior knowledge and understanding.

Learning is a social process

Provision needs to be made in teaching situations for social interaction and discussion in pairs and other groups of varying sizes, both with and without the teacher taking part. The tradition of learning as a process of discussion can be traced back to Plato and Aristotle, but, for a great many years in the more recent history of education, discussion and collaboration have not been encouraged. There are certainly times when children should work quietly and alone, but there are many more occasions when to enter into a dialogue is extremely valuable (Little 1995). The work of Vygotsky and Bruner, in particular, and of others, including Bandura, has shown that learning is a process of interaction between learners. The interaction between learner and a 'more knowledgeable other' is an important aspect of scaffolding, as is interaction between peers.

Teachers being in dialogue with children, in both whole-class situations and in other groupings, including one-to-one conversations, forms the basis of much good teaching. Different phases of lessons are based to greater and lesser extents on the use of talk, by the teacher but also by the learner. In some lessons, there is a phase of exposition, where a teacher takes on the role of provider of information. This can be a one-way process, but, when it involves two-way interaction, it is likely to be more effective. The use of focused questioning – particularly, the use of different styles of question – should form a part of a teacher's repertoire of approaches to their job. Teachers need to understand and be able to use different types of questions. Using only 'closed' questions, requiring simple one-word answers, will not serve any purpose as far as the elicitation of children's ideas is concerned. Other, more facilitating types of questions should be employed.

Possibly more important than the times when a teacher is in direct dialogue with groups or individuals are the times when lessons move into a more independent phase; that is, the teacher takes on a less obvious role and children are expected to work under a lower level of supervision from the teacher. During this phase, children can certainly be asked to work individually, but, if the opportunity to work collaboratively, in groups of different sizes, is not taken, then important learning opportunities are missed. There is a difference between sitting in groups, and working individually, and actively working together. Collaborative work implies that there is a shared task that is to be worked on together; either at a simple level, by discussing the topic and then responding separately, or at a more sophisticated level, working together to arrive at a collaborative solution or joint end product. For this to be effective, children need support in learning how to discuss and how to collaborate. Tasks need to be succinct, achievable and within the capabilities of the group. Often, what we can call the learning styles needs of the individual class members need to be taken into account, too. Sensitive teachers will take great care when forming groups and will give opportunities for some children to work alone on occasions. This being said, it is important to give opportunities to learn how to work collaboratively and co-operatively to those who find it difficult. The teacher's role in dealing with this is not straightforward.

There is research to show that the benefits of group work can be great. Mercer (2000), for example, gives a detailed account of the ways in which language can be a medium for effective learning.

In online distance learning situations, dialogue is considered as an essential element of the process of learning. Synchronous (in real time) and asynchronous (exchanges taking place over an extended time period) discussion through the medium of computer conferencing are built into the programme of learning in most online courses mediated by information technology. Although this is not directly applicable in most school learning situations, the importance of social contact and dialogue is underlined.

Learning is situated

Teaching does not take place in a vacuum, and all of the parties involved – teachers, children, curriculum and resource developers, and more – bring their own contextual concerns. The context in which learning takes place influences the effectiveness of the learning. A learning context can be analysed in terms of its culture – its values, beliefs and commonly agreed standards. The context can also be analysed in terms of the time of day, the prevailing weather conditions and the immediate physical surroundings. Between these two extremities of definition of context lies a set of important considerations that teachers should take into account. These considerations are to do with the breadth of experience that children bring with them to their learning. Meaningful contexts for learning are very important, and it must be remembered that what is meaningful for a teacher is not necessarily meaningful for the child.

Something as simple as using a map of the school or the immediate local environment for an introductory lesson on maps, directions or routes can, in some cases, lead to far more engagement in the work, and, therefore, an increase in the likelihood of learning taking place, than if a random or fictitious map is used. When particular work is not progressing as well as had been anticipated, a teacher can always ask a question about the 'setting' of the work, and establish if it might be possible to set the underlying knowledge and concepts in a more generally child-friendly setting. Simple modifications can make big differences.

The customisation of resources is one way of attempting to deal with this concern. For example, putting a set of mathematical problems into the context of a children's television programme that is currently watched by the class can help to stimulate both interest and understanding. (The word 'currently' is important here, because a programme that was aired even as recently as five years ago might as well be from a hundred years ago as far as primary school-aged children are concerned.) Another simple approach that can be taken is to use the context of a story that the children are currently reading together, or have recently experienced, and to make use of text from the story to exemplify particular aspects of language that are being learnt. A page from a favourite book with all of the adjectives missing, for example, can have an interest level and wider appeal to a class of children who have read the book far beyond that of another, comparatively arbitrary piece of text.

Learning is a metacognitive process

A good example of how a consideration of a learning process might be of value to learners is when a class might be asked to learn a list of spellings. (Sadly, many spelling lists, which lack the context that might help the process of learning, are presented for learning simply because they are the next set from the 'list'.) For many children, learning spellings is very difficult. If they are not given any guidance in how to learn them, the task can become impossible. There are many different approaches that can be taken, and suggested to children, for learning spellings. Since any given class of children will have a range of different learning preferences represented, it is a sound approach to offer a set of different suggestions. A good starting point might be to ask the class how they go about learning a list. Some children will not have an approach; others will. As we saw earlier, the approaches taken will vary widely, in all probability, from such suggestions as 'I look at the word and photograph it in my brain, then I know it' to 'I write it out ten times as fast as I can and it sticks in my head' or 'I make up sentences for them and I can remember the sentences then with the words in them'. Simply talking about approaches to this type of learning can make a difference to some children who struggle to learn the words each week. Those who struggle can be asked to devise a way of learning that they will find helpful; it can be based on suggestions from the teacher or on ideas suggested by others in the class. Another way of encouraging thought about learning or mental processing is to ask children to explain how they know something or how they worked it out. In the context of mental arithmetic, for example, listening to explanations of how an answer was arrived at can be an illuminating experience – for both the teacher and the rest of the class alike.

As children get older and the demands made of them increase – in terms of preparation for exams, for example – the approaches that can be taken to revision, and a detailed consideration of what will work best for them individually, become important. An awareness of how best to tackle what can be daunting learning or revising tasks can help to ease the apparent burden. This is true at all levels.

Children's awareness of their own learning, their thought processes, should be promoted. By promoting this awareness, teachers are encouraging metacognitive activity.

Learning can sometimes proceed in a rote fashion, with little understanding involved

This is, perhaps, a controversial position to take. What this does not mean is that memorising is the key to learning, which is far from the truth. Understanding should be the aim of education. However, if not 'knowing' certain items of information becomes a hindrance in the process of learning, it can be acceptable to 'drill' the information, in the hope and expectation that, with subsequent, well-focused teaching and experience, understanding will follow. Ideally, teachers would like young children to know multiplication facts and to understand what it is that they are dealing with. Actually understanding what is meant by 'five threes are 15' is important. Knowing that it could refer to three groups of five or to five groups of three (leading to an understanding of the commutativity of multiplication) and knowing how to work out the answer to the question, 'What is three times five?', should the need arise, is also very important. Having the ability to apply the multiplication fact in a problem with money is something that teachers would also expect. However, if a child struggles to understand, or if understanding progresses slowly and with difficulty, actually being able to respond instantly with the answer '15' in a situation where the result of the multiplication is needed to help towards solving a more advanced problem (concerning area, perhaps) is a very useful ability.

The same can apply in a range of situations in different subject areas. Understanding should be the aim, but recall can be accepted as a valuable halfway house in some cases.

Learning can sometimes depend on an individual's preferred learning style

When considering the different preferred styles that individual learners might have, or when taking into account the manifold possibilities when thinking about multiple intelligence profiles, a teacher could be excused for deciding that there are too many variables and too many diverse needs to be met. This is indeed the case, but teachers do need to take into account the needs of the learners in their classes. One of the questions that arises in discussions about learning style and multiple intelligence centres on whether a teacher should match learning tasks to the supposed needs of each learner, or whether each learner should be encouraged to widen their learning strategy horizon. Or, in terms of multiple intelligences, the question centres on whether a learner with a particular multiple intelligence strength should be taught with that strength in mind, to the exclusion of approaches that make demands on other intelligences, or should teaching attempt to engage the less strong areas of intelligence in an attempt to strengthen them? The answers to questions of this nature are not easy.

Some would take an extreme position and say that learners with, for example, a kinaesthetic learning propensity should be taught in ways that allow the learner to adopt this style of learning and no other. Some would argue that a learner with high logical intelligence and low linguistic intelligence should have teaching and learning approaches that are aimed at the latter in order that the learner might 'improve' in this area. The result of this particular approach could be that this particular learner fails to learn in an effective manner.

There is a modern parable written by George Reavis (2000) entitled 'The Animal School'. It relates a time when animals formed their own school with a curriculum of flying, running and swimming. Those who excelled in any one of the core subjects were given additional teaching in the other subjects, and, so, the duck was made to spend his time practising running to the point where he became a poor swimmer as a result of the damage caused to his feet. Other animals had similar unfortunate experiences. The animals were obliged to work in the way prescribed and exceptions were not allowed. Any individual strengths or preferences were not taken into account, with the result that most of the animal pupils failed. There are resonances with the parable and the ways in which some formal education is organised, especially in the past, but also, we could perhaps say, in classrooms where what is known about learning styles and multiple intelligences is not taken into account.

In a class of 30 or more pupils, it would be very difficult to cater adequately, in every lesson on every day, for each and every individual need. It is sometimes a big enough problem dealing with differentiation in terms of levels of ability in a large and diverse classroom without also providing highly differentiated activities to suit all learning styles and intelligence profiles. So, what would a sensible teaching approach look like?

It is generally accepted that teachers should have an understanding of learning style and related areas of interest, and that this knowledge should impact on the ways that teachers plan and teach. Taking into account the difficulties of working with an approach that gives priority to learning style (some of which are considered above), teachers need to provide opportunities for all children to work with their preferred style and within the domain of their intelligence profile of strengths. This will mean allowing for varied approaches at different times, and it will also mean allowing for a certain amount of choice on the part of the learners, concerning how they tackle particular tasks and also in how they respond to certain 'requirements' of the teaching.

Some of these choices may appear simple and even trivial, but for some learners they can make a significant difference to the progress of their learning.

Choice of activity

- Work alone or work with a partner.
- Gather information from books (text or diagrams, tables of statistics), the Internet; an audio recording of a radio programme, a video recording of a television programme.
- Complete a worksheet.
- Solve a problem related to the topic.

Choice of response

- Individual response or a group response.
- Respond in note form, prose, diagrams or pictures.
- Respond in the form of a creative narrative, even for science in some circumstances.
- Respond in the form of a three-dimensional model.
- Respond in the form of an audio-recorded news item.
- Respond in the form of a video diary.
- Produce and deliver a short presentation (with or without the use of ICT).
- Create a dramatic piece for performance.

All of the above-suggested choices relate to one or other learning style preference or multiple intelligence, to greater or lesser degrees. They also are to be found in classrooms in schools throughout the country – there is nothing new in these two lists. However, it is possible that some teachers do not provide a range of different options in their teaching. If, for example, a class is always asked to break into groups of three and discuss the topic in question before responding orally to the rest of the class, a proportion of individual children will be advantaged, in terms of their access to the lesson, and others disadvantaged. If the response expected to any given work on any given topic is always an individual piece of writing, with a diagram or picture if there is time, the same situation of advantage and disadvantage will exist. Teachers do not need to switch from one approach to another on a roundabout of confusion, but they should be fully aware of the need to cater for the wide range of interests, abilities, propensities and intelligences that will be present in their classrooms. Giving options for ways of working, and for what are sometimes called 'end products', or 'recording', is one way of doing this.

It is very likely that the predominant means of response to a task will remain individual and be in a standard written form. This is a result of the nature of our current educational system, which will change only very slowly, and teachers do need to prepare their pupils for what is expected of them, either in the exam system in later years of education or in adult life. But, if learning is to progress in as effective a way as possible, and for as many of our young learners as possible, then choice and variety need to be a part of what is offered to them.

Learning can be affected by certain conditions concerning the brain

Firstly, it seems clear that an emotionally stable environment in which trusting and respectful relationships exist is a desirable point of departure. Heightened emotions, especially to do with fun, enjoyment, excitement and, possibly, a low level of worry (about wanting to succeed, finish what is expected and wanting to please the teacher) seem to serve the aim of promoting effective learning. We know that this is a difficult state of affairs to establish and maintain, but it could be an aspiration to achieve it for at least some of the time, perhaps. That is to say that not all lessons can be new and exciting, but many can be; also, a relaxed and well-prepared teacher (also an important aspiration in some cases) can lead to a relaxed atmosphere in which trusting relationships can begin to be built.

At the very least, it seems that, to be receptive to teaching and to be effective learners, we need to be well rested, well ventilated and well nourished, including having an adequate supply of water. We can talk either in terms of what the learner needs or what the brain needs, in this case. To supply some of these needs is within the gift of the school. Schools cannot impose bedtimes, nor can they ensure healthy diets (though they can teach about them), but water and oxygen can be supplied very easily: water in the form of access and encouragement, and oxygen in the form of good ventilation and movement of one sort or another.

Teachers can aim to achieve 'relaxed alertness' in their pupils by the ways in which they organise their teaching and classrooms and the ways in which they respond to their pupils. Teachers can consider what is meant by 'orchestrated immersion' and make decisions about how to best fit this requirement into the experiences that they provide. They can also encourage, by the nature of the tasks they set, the 'active processing' and engagement with facts and ideas that form the core of what it is that they want their pupils to learn.

Based on what we have considered above and in earlier chapters, we can devise a checklist of points that a teacher might consider when planning lessons.

Lesson checklist

- Is there a clear focus, with explicit learning objectives?
- Is the content based on, and intended to build upon, the pupils' existing knowledge?
- Is the lesson set in an appropriate context?
- Is there scope for social interaction and for activity?
- Is there variety and choice involved in approaches and responses to work?
- Is the lesson planned in such a way that it aims to move the pupils' learning forward?

Naturally, all lessons will be different. There will be occasions when there is, for example, little opportunity for collaborative work, or limited scope for assuring that the social or cultural context is ideal for the class in question. However, efforts can be made and steps taken to work towards meeting the conditions implied by this list. All lessons need to have a clear focus and aims. Ideally, these aims should be made clear to the class. In situations where work continues from one lesson to the next, an opportunity to refresh the aims in the minds of the class should be taken. All lessons should, in some way, have the purpose of moving on knowledge and understanding; even lessons that are for the purpose of revision can be seen to be moving on and revitalising what has been covered before.

If what has been discovered about effective learning is applied in classrooms, teachers will plan and work in a different way from that which has become established practice over a large number of years. Teaching approaches will be tailored to what is known about learning and will encompass what has been discovered in recent years about learning and the brain. This will lead to a new learning environment in the classroom, when compared with what has gone before. Cohen *et al.* (2010) describe the differences between a more traditional setting and a new, restructured setting, as set out in Table 8.2.

TABLE 8.2 Conventional and restructured teaching settings

	Conventional setting	*Restructured setting*
Pupil role	Learn facts and skills by absorbing the content presented by teachers and media resources.	Create knowledge by acting on content provided by teachers, media resources and personal experiences.
Curriculum characteristics	Fragmented knowledge and disciplinary separation. Basic literacy established before higher order-level enquiry is encouraged. Focus on breadth of knowledge.	Multidisciplinary themes, knowledge integration and application. Emphasis on thinking skills and application. Emphasis on depth of understanding.
Social characteristics	Teacher-controlled setting with pupils working independently. Some competition.	Teacher functions as facilitator and learner. Pupils work collaboratively and make some decisions.
Assessment	Measurement of fact knowledge and discrete skills. Traditional tests.	Assessment of knowledge application. Performance of tasks to demonstrate understanding.
Teacher role	Present information and manage classroom.	Guide pupil enquiry and model active learning.

(Continued)

TABLE 8.2 Continued

	Conventional setting	Restructured setting
Possible use of the Internet	Source of information for absorption.	Source of information for interpretation and knowledge construction. Outlet for original work.
'Brain-based' and learning style considerations	Very few in evidence; emphasis on listening, reading and writing.	Movement around class encouraged; consideration of pupils' concentration span; variety in approach taken by teacher; choice in response encouraged.

Source: Cohen *et al.* 2004, with minor additions

'Excellence' and 'enjoyment' – the two words in the title of the UK Government's policy for developing the work of primary schools (DfES 2003) – sum up what schools can aim for. (Despite the fact that this document is no longer current, it still has a good deal to offer.) Children can achieve excellence and, in the process, derive satisfaction and enjoyment from their work. The excellence may well be a personal excellence and should, perhaps, be seen as achieving potential, but the enjoyment can be real for them when they are allowed and encouraged to work in appropriate ways in a school and classroom atmosphere that supports learning and is prepared and maintained by teachers who are aware of the important considerations concerning learning that we have examined in this book. Learning depends on, and demands, a certain amount of work on the part of the learner. Teachers, by applying what is known about learning and developing rich learning experiences based on prior knowledge, social interaction and metacognitive ideas, in appropriate contexts and taking into account various conditions considered to be beneficial to effective learning, are in a privileged position. They are able to take a very strong lead in the process of helping children to reach their potential whilst at the same time enjoying themselves.

Appendix

Comparing and contrasting Piaget and Vygotsky – in summary

Both were constructivists

Both Piaget and Vygotsky believed that individuals actively construct their own knowledge and understanding; Vygotsky stressed the importance of the social interaction in which an individual participates; Piaget stressed the inner motivation to balance new information with existing knowledge and understanding.

Vygotsky	Piaget
Social constructivism	Cognitive constructivism
Children learn through being active.	Children learn through being active.
Learning is a socially mediated activity.	Children operate as 'lone scientists'.
Emphasis placed on the role of the teacher or 'more knowledgeable other' as a 'scaffolder'.	If a child is shown how to do something rather than being encouraged to discover it for themselves, understanding may actually be inhibited.
The teacher is a facilitator who provides the challenges that the child needs for achieving more.	The teacher is the provider of 'artefacts' needed for the child to work with and learn from.

(continued)

Vygotsky	Piaget
Development is fostered by collaboration (in the 'zone of proximal development'), and not strictly age related.	Cognitive growth has a biological, age-related, developmental basis.
Development is an internalisation of social experience; with appropriate support, children can be taught concepts that are just beyond their level of development. 'What the child can do with an adult today, they can do alone tomorrow.'	Children are unable to extend their cognitive capabilities beyond their stage of development. There is no point in teaching a concept that is beyond their current stage of development.

References

Bandler, R. and Grinder, J. (1979) *Frogs into princes: neuro linguistic programming*. Moab, UT: Real People Press.

Bandura, A. (1977) *Social learning theory*. Englewood Cliffs, NJ: Prentice-Hall.

BDA (British Dyslexia Association) (2008) *Dyslexia research information* [online]. Available at: http://www.bdadyslexia.org.uk (accessed 18.03.13).

BDA (2009) BDA definition of dyslexia. In: *Dyslexia research information* [online]. Available at: http://www.bdadyslexia.org.uk/about-dyslexia/further-information/dyslexia-research-information-.html (accessed 23.04.13).

Becker, H. J. (1993) A model for improving the performance of integrated learning systems: mixed individualized/group/whole class lessons, cooperative learning, and organizing time for teacher-led remediation of small groups. In: G. D. Bailey (ed.), *Computer-based integrated learning systems*. Englewood Cliffs, NJ: Educational Technology Publications.

Bereiter, C. and Scardamalia, M. (1987) *The psychology of written composition*. Hillsdale, NJ: Lawrence Erlbaum Associates.

BPS (British Psychological Society) (1999) *Dyslexia, literacy and psychological assessment*. Leicester: BPS.

Bricheno, P. and Younger, M. (2004) Some unexpected results of learning styles intervention? In: British Educational Research Association (BERA), *BERA Annual Conference*, UMIST, Manchester, 16–18 September 2004.

Briggs Myers, I. and Myers, P. B. (1980) *Gifts differing*. Palo Alto: Consulting Psychologists Press.

Briggs, K. and Briggs Myers, I. (1975) *The Myers-Briggs Type Indicator*. Palo Alto, CA: Consulting Psychologists Press.

Brown, A. (1987) Metacognition, executive control, self-regulation, and other more mysterious mechanisms. In: F. E. Weinert and R. H. Kluwe (eds), *Metacognition, motivation, and understanding* (3rd edn). Hillsdale, NJ: Lawrence Erlbaum Associates.

Brown, J. S., Collins, A. and Duguid, P. (1989) Situated cognition and the culture of learning, *Educational Researcher*, 18(1), 32–42.

Bruer, J. T. (1997) Education and the brain: a bridge too far, *Educational Researcher*, 26(8), 4–16.

Bruner, J. S. (1996) *The culture of education*. Cambridge, MA: Harvard University Press.

Caine, R. N. and Caine, G. (1994) *Making connections: teaching and the human brain*. Somerset, NJ: Addison Wesley.

Caine, R. N. and Caine, G. (1997) *Unleashing the power of perceptual change: the potential of brain-based teaching*. Alexandria, VA: Association for Supervision and Curriculum Development.

Campbell, B. and Campbell, L. (1993) Learning through the multiple intelligences, *Intelligence Connections*, Fall. Available at: http://www.multi-intell.com/articles/campbell_ article.htm (accessed 03.01.05).

Carle, E. (2002) (1st edn, 1969) *The very hungry caterpillar*. London: Puffin Books.

Chandler, D. (1984) *Young learners and the microcomputer*. Milton Keynes: Open University Press.

Chastain, K. (1971) *The development of modern language skills: theory to practice*. Chicago, IL: Rand McNally.

Cockcroft, W. H.; Committee of Inquiry into the Teaching of Mathematics in Schools, Great Britain (1982) *Mathematics counts* (Cockcroft report). London: HMSO.

Coffield, F., Moseley, D., Hall, E. and Ecclestone, K. (2004a) *Learning styles and pedagogy in post-16 learning: a systematic and critical review*. London: Learning and Skills Research Centre.

Coffield, F., Moseley, D., Hall, E. and Ecclestone, K. (2004b) *Should we be using learning styles? What research has to say to practice*. London: Learning and Skills Research Centre.

Cohen, L., Manion, L. and Morrison, K. (2004) *A guide to teaching practice* (5th edn). London: Routledge.

Crisfield, J. (ed.) (1996) *The dyslexia handbook*. Reading: British Dyslexia Association.

Curran, A. and Gilbert, I. (ed.) (2008) *The little book of big stuff about the brain: the true story of your amazing brain*. Carmarthen: Crown Publishing.

Davis, P. M. (1991) *Cognition and learning: a review of the literature with reference to ethnolinguistic minorities*. Dallas, TX: Summer Institute of Linguistics.

Della Valle, J., Dunn, R., Dunn, K., Geisert, G., Sinatra, R. and Zenhausern, R. (1986) The effects of matching and mismatching students' mobility preferences on recognition and memory tasks, *Journal of Educational Research*, 79(5), 267–72.

Demetriou, A., Shayer, M. and Efklides, A. (eds) (1992) *Neo-Piagetian theories of cognitive development: implications and applications for education* (International Library of Psychology series). London, New York: Routledge.

DES (Department of Education and Science) (1985) *The curriculum from 5 to 16* (HMI series: Curriculum matters, no. 2). London: HMSO.

Dewar, T. (1996) *Adult learning online* [online]. Available at http://www.cybercorp.net/ tammy/lo/oned2.html (accessed 11.11.04).

DfE (Department for Education) (2012a) School Direct. In: *Initial teaching training* [online]. Available at http://www.education.gov.uk/schools/careers/training anddevelopment/initial/b00205704/schooldirect (accessed 12.03.13).

DfE (2012b) *Teachers' standards*. Available at https://www.gov.uk/government/publications/teachers-standards (accessed 12.03.13).

DfEE (Department for Education and Employment) (2000a) *Code of practice on the assessment of pupils with special educational needs (SEN) and SEN thresholds: good practice guidance on identification and provision for pupils with special educational needs* (draft) [consultation document]. Available at: https://www.education.gov.uk/consultations/index.cfm?action=conResults&consultationId=1077&external=no&menu=3 (accessed 15.04.08; 12.03.13).

DfEE (2000b) Access to basic skills for people with dyslexia. In: *Freedom to learn: basic skills for learners with learning difficulties and/or disabilities*, Report of the working group looking into the basic skills needed for adults with learning difficulties and/or disabilities, May 2000. Available at: http://www.lifelonglearning.co.uk/freedomtolearn/rep08.htm (accessed 20.04.13).

DfES (Department for Education and Skills) (2003) *Excellence and enjoyment: a strategy for primary schools*. London: DfES.

Diamond, M. C., Scheibel, A. B. and Elson, L. M. (1986) *The human brain coloring book.* New York, NY: HarperCollins.

Draper, S. W. (2012) *Learning styles (notes)* [online], Department of Psychology, University of Glasgow. Available at: http://www.psy.gla.ac.uk/ steve/lstyles.html (accessed 14.03.13).

Drubach, D. (2000) *The brain explained.* Upper Saddle River, NJ: Prentice-Hall.

DSA (Down's Syndrome Association) (2013) What is the incidence of Down's Syndrome? In: *Down's Syndrome Association – general FAQs* [online]. Available at: http://www.downs-syndrome.org.uk/about-us/key-facts-and-faqs/faqs/general-faqs.html (accessed 14.03.13).

Dunn, R. S. and Dunn, K. (1978) *Teaching students through their individual learning styles: a practical approach.* Reston, VA: Reston Publishing Company.

Dunn, R. S., Cavanaugh, D., Eberle, B. and Zenhausern, R. (1982) Hemispheric preference: the newest element of learning style, *The American Biology Teacher,* 44(5), 291–4.

Dunn, R. S., Dunn, K. J. and Price, G. E. (1989) *The learning style inventory: an inventory for the identification of how individuals in grades 3 through 12 prefer to learn.* Lawrence, KS: Price Systems.

Dyslexia Institute Limited (2008) *Dyslexia Action* website [online]. Available at: http://www.dyslexiaaction.org.uk (accessed 20.04.08).

EC (European Commission) (2012) FP7: the future of European Union research policy. In: *European Commission – Research & Innovation* [online]. Available at: http://ec.europa.eu/research/fp7/index_en.cfm (accessed 21.04.13).

Elliott, S. N. and Busse, R. T. (1991) Social skills assessment and intervention with children and adolescents: guidelines for assessment and training procedures, *School Psychology International,* 12(1–2), 63–83.

Ellis, A. (1973) *Humanistic psychotherapy.* New York, NY: Julian Press.

Felder, R. M. and Silverman, L. K. (1988) Learning and teaching styles in engineering education. *Engineering Education,* 78(7): 674–81.

Flavell, J. H. (1976) Metacognitive aspects of problem solving. In: L. B. Resnick (ed.); Learning Research and Development Center, University of Pittsburgh, *The nature of intelligence.* Hillsdale, NJ: Lawrence Erlbaum Associates.

Flavell, J. H. (1977) *Cognitive development.* Englewood Cliffs, NJ: Prentice-Hall.

Fleming, N. D. (2001) *Teaching and learning styles: VARK strategies.* Christchurch, New Zealand: Neil Fleming.

Frith, U. (1999) Paradoxes in the definition of dyslexia, *Dyslexia,* 5(4), 192–214.

Fuchs, K. L. (2009) Team focus: neuropsychologist, *International Journal of MS Care,* 11(1), 32–7.

Gardner, H. (1983) *Frames of mind: the theory of multiple intelligences.* New York, NY: Basic Books.

Gardner, H. (1993) *Multiple intelligences: the theory in practice.* New York, NY: Basic Books.

Gardner, H. and Hatch, T. (1990) *Multiple intelligences go to school: educational implications of the theory of multiple intelligences,* Center for Technology in Education (CTE) Report no. 4 (TR4), March 1990. Available at: http://www.edc.org/cct/ccthome/reports/tr4.html (accessed 12.03.13).

Gigglepotz (2000) Multiple intelligences: lesson plans [online]. Available at: http://www.gigglepotz.com/miplans.htm (accessed 30.1.05).

Gilbert, I. (2008) In: A. Curran and I. Gilbert (ed.), *The little book of big stuff about the brain: the true story of your amazing brain.* Carmarthen: Crown House Publishing.

Goleman, D. (1998) *Working with emotional intelligence.* London: Bloomsbury.

Gopnik, A. and Meltzoff, A. (1997) *Words, thoughts, and theories.* Cambridge MA: MIT Press.

Green, H.; Office for National Statistics, Department of Health and the Scottish Executive (2005) *Mental health of children and young people in Great Britain, 2004.* Basingstoke: Palgrave Macmillan. Available at: http://www.esds.ac.uk/doc/5269/mrdoc/pdf/5269technicalreport.pdf [accessed 10.05.13].

Greenfield, S. (2005) Answer rich, question poor? *Times Educational Supplement*, 28 January 2005. Available online at: http://www.tes.co.uk/article.aspx?storycode=2069110 (accessed 21.03.13).

Hartman, V. (1995) Teaching and learning style preferences: transitions through technology, *VCCA Journal*, 9(2), 18–20.

Hastings, S. (2012) Learning styles. *Times Educational Supplement*, 10 December 2012. Available online at: http://www.tes.co.uk/article.aspx?storycode=2153773 (accessed 21.03.13).

Hay/McBer; DfEE (2000) *Research into teacher effectiveness: a model of teacher effectiveness*, Research report no. 216. London: DfEE.

Heilman, K. M. and Gilmore, R. L. (1998) Cortical influences in emotion, *Journal of Clinical Neurophysiology*, 15(5), 409–23.

Hoerr, T. R. (1996) *Celebrating multiple intelligences: teaching for success.* St Louis, MO: New City School.

Holland, J. H., Holyoak, K. J., Nisbett, R. E. and Thagard, P. R. (1986) *Induction: processes of inference, learning and discovery.* Cambridge, MA: MIT Press.

Honey, P. and Mumford, A. (1986) *Manual of learning styles* (2nd edn). Maidenhead, Berkshire: P. Honey.

Howard-Jones, P. (2011) From brain scan to lesson plan, *The Psychologist*, 24(2), 110–13.

Howard-Jones, P., Franey, L., Mashmoushi, R. and Liao, Y-C. (2009) The neuroscience literacy of trainee teachers. In: British Educational Research Association (BERA), *BERA Annual Conference*, University of Manchester, 2–5 September 2009.

Howe, M. J. A. (1999) *A teacher's guide to the psychology of learning.* London: Blackwell.

Hunter, J.; Autism Working Group (2006) *Autistic spectrum disorders: a guide to classroom practice.* Guidance produced by the Autism Working Group, the Education and Training Inspectorate (ETI), and the Department of Education, Northern Ireland (DENI). Belfast: DENI. Available at: http://www.etini.gov.uk/asd_classroom_practice.pdf (accessed 30.04.08).

James, W. (1890) *The principles of psychology.* New York, NY: Henry Holt.

Jensen, E. (1998) *Teaching with the brain in mind.* London: Atlantic Books.

Johnson, A. and Kuntz, S. (1997) And the survey says . . . how teachers use the theory of multiple intelligences, *Classroom Leadership*, 1(1). Available at: http://www.ascd.org/publications/classroom-leadership/sept1997/And-the-Survey-Says. . .-How-Teachers-Use-the-Theory-of-Multiple-Intelligences.aspx (accessed 03.01.05).

Johnson-Laird, P. N. (1983) *Mental models: towards a cognitive science of language, inference, and consciousness.* Cambridge, MA: Harvard University Press.

Jonassen, D. H., Peck, K. L. and Wilson, B. G. (1999) *Learning with technology: a constructivist perspective.* Upper Saddle River, NJ: Merrill.

Karmiloff-Smith, A. (1992) *Beyond modularity: a developmental perspective on cognitive science.* Cambridge, MA: MIT Press.

Kearsley, G. (n.d.) Multiple intelligences (Howard Gardner). In: *Learning Theories*, Theory into Practice (TIP) guides, InstructionalDesign.org [online]. Available at: http://tip.psychology.org/gardner.html (accessed 22.01.13).

Killion, K. (1999; 2002) Review: *Teaching with the brain in mind* by Eric Jensen, Association for Supervision and Curriculum Development (ASCD). In: *Illinois Loop*, 25 January 1999. Available at: http://www.illinoisloop.org/twbim.html (accessed 21.01.05).

Kolb, D. A. (1984) *Experiential learning: experience as the source of learning and development.* Englewood Cliffs, NJ: Prentice-Hall.

Kolb, D. A. and Fry, R. E. (1974) *Toward an applied theory of experiential learning,* Sloan School of Management series. Cambridge, MA: MIT Press.

Lave, J. and Wenger, E. (1991) *Situated learning: legitimate peripheral participation.* Cambridge: Cambridge University Press.

Leadership Project (1995) *Adult Learning Principles and Practice.* Toronto: Sheridan College.

Lee, J. (2013) Open your mind to the teachings of neuroscience. *Times Educational Supplement,* 1 March 2013. Available at: http://www.tes.co.uk/article.aspx?storycode=6322171 [accessed 10.05.13].

Lemmon, P. (1985) A school where learning styles make a difference, *Principal,* 64, 26–9.

Levine, M. (2002) *The myth of laziness.* New York, NY: Simon and Schuster.

Levine, M. (2003) *A mind at a time.* New York, NY: Simon and Schuster.

Little, D. (1995) Learning as dialogue: the dependence of learner autonomy on teacher autonomy, *System,* 23(2), 175–81.

McFarlane, A. E. (1997) Thinking about writing. In: A. E. McFarlane (ed.), *Information technology and authentic learning.* London: Routledge.

MacLean, P. (1974) *Triune conception of the brain and behaviour.* Toronto, Canada: University of Toronto Press.

MacLean, P. (1989) *The triune brain in evolution: role in palaeocerebral functions.* Dordrecht, The Netherlands: Kluwer Academic.

MacMurren, H. (1985) A comparative study of the effects of matching and mismatching sixth-grade students with their learning style preferences for the physical element of intake and their subsequent reading speed and accuracy scores and attitudes. Ph.D. dissertation, St. John's University, New York, 1985.

Mason, J. and Steenhuysen, J. (2013) Obama launches research initiative to study human brain. In: Reuters.com (U.S. edition) [online]. Available at: http://www.reuters.com/article/2013/04/02/us-obama-brain-idUSBRE9310H820130402 (accessed 20.04.13).

Massa, L. J. and Mayer, R. E. (2006) Testing the ATI hypothesis: should multimedia instruction accommodate verbalizer–visualizer cognitive style?, *Learning and Individual Differences,* 16(4), 321–36.

Mayer, R. E. (1983) *Thinking: problem solving and cognition.* New York, NY: W. H. Freeman & Co.

Mercer, N. (2000) *Words and minds: how we use language to think together.* London: Routledge.

Minsky, M. L. (1986) *The society of mind.* Simon and Schuster, New York.

NAS (National Autistic Society) (2008) *National Autistic Society* website [online]. Available at: http://www.autism.org.uk (accessed 16.03.13).

O'Keefe, J. and Nadel, L. (1978) *The hippocampus as a cognitive map.* New York, NY: Oxford University Press.

Ogle, D. M. (1989) The 'know, want to know, learn' strategy. In: K. D. Muth (ed.), *Children's comprehension of text: research into practice.* Newark, DE: International Reading Association.

Pashler, H., McDaniel, M., Rohrer, D. and Bjork, R. (2009) Learning styles: concepts and evidence, *Psychological Science in the Public Interest,* 9(3), 105–19.

Poole, C. R. (1997) Maximising learning: a conversation with Renate Nummela Caine, *Educational Leadership,* 54(6), 11–15.

Posner, M. I. (ed.) (1984) *Foundations of cognitive science.* Cambridge, MA: MIT Press.

Pritchard, A. and Woollard, J. (2010) *Psychology for the classroom: constructivism and social learning.* London: Routledge.

Purcell, I. (n.d.) *Integrated learning systems – do they enhance learning?* Available at: http://www.cbltwork.soton.ac.uk/purcell/prin/&gse;ction2 (accessed 01.12.04).

Ravitch, D. (2000) Hard lessons. In: *Atlantic Unbound (Atlantic Monthly)* [online], 1 November 2000.

Reavis, G. H. (2000) The Animal School. In: J. Canfield and M. V. Hansen (eds), *Chicken soup for the soul: stories that restore your faith in human nature*. London: Vermilion.

Reid, J., Forrestal, P. and Cook, J. (1989) *Small group learning in the classroom*. Scarborough, Australia: Chalkface Press; London: English and Media Centre.

Reid-Lyon, G. (1995) Toward a definition of dyslexia, *Annals of Dyslexia*, 45(1), 1–27.

Richardson, J. and Joughin, C. (2002) *Parent training programmes for the management of young children with conduct disorders: findings from research*. London: Royal College of Psychiatrists.

Rose, C. P. and Nicholl, M. J. (1997) *Accelerated learning for the 21st century: the six-step plan to unlock your master-mind*. New York, NY: Dell Publishing.

Rose, J. (2009) *Identifying and teaching children and young people with dyslexia and literacy difficulties: an independent report from Sir Jim Rose to the Secretary of State for Children, Schools and Families*, June 2009. Nottingham: DCSF Publications.

Royer, J. M. (ed.) (2005) *The cognitive revolution in educational psychology* Charlotte, NC: Information Age Publishing.

Ruggiero, V. R. (2000) *The art of thinking: a guide to critical and creative thought* (6th edn). New York, NY: Pearson Longman.

Salovey, P. and Mayer, J. D. (1990) Emotional intelligence, *Imagination, Cognition and Personality*, 9(3), 185–211.

Selinger, M. (2001) Setting authentic tasks using the Internet in schools. In: M. Leask (ed.), *Issues in teaching using ICT*. London: Routledge Falmer.

Sewell, D. (1990) *New tools for new minds: a cognitive perspective on the use of computers with young children*. Hemel Hempstead: Harvester Wheatsheaf.

Skinner, B. F. (1958) Reinforcement today, *American Psychologist*, 13(3), 94–9.

Spoon, J. C. and Schell, J. W. (1998) Aligning student learning styles with instructor teaching styles. *Journal of Industrial Teacher Education*, 35(2), 41–56.

Stahl, S. A. (2002) Different strokes for different folks? In: L. Abbeduto (ed.), *Taking sides: clashing on controversial issues in educational psychology* (2nd edn). Guilford, CT: Dushkin/McGraw-Hill.

Stanovich, K. E. (1996) Toward a more inclusive definition of dyslexia, *Dyslexia*, 2(3), 154–66.

Stokes, G. and Whiteside, D. (1984) *Basic one brain: dyslexic learning correction and brain integration*. Burbank, CA: Three In One Concepts.

TDA (Training and Development Agency) (2007) Professional standards for teachers. London: TDA.

Tomblin, J. B., Records, N. L., Buckwalter, P., Zhang, X., Smith, E. and O'Brien, M. (1997). Prevalence of specific language impairment in kindergarten children. *Journal of Speech Language Hearing Research.*, 40(6), 1245–60.

Underwood, J. D. M. and Brown, J. (eds); National Council for Educational Technology (1997) *Integrated learning systems: potential into practice*. Oxford: Heinemann.

Underwood, J. D. M., Cavendish, S., Dowling, S., Fogelman, K. and Lawson, T. (1994) *Integrated learning systems in UK schools: final report*. Coventry: National Council for Educational Technology; Leicester: School of Education, University of Leicester.

Waites, L.; World Federation of Neurology (1968) Specific developmental dyslexia. In: *Report of the Research Group of Developmental Dyslexia of the World Federation of Neurology*.

Wing, L. and Gould, J. (1979) Severe impairments of social interaction and associated abnormalities in children: epidemiology and classification, *Journal of Autism and Developmental Disorders*, 9(1), 11–29.

Woolfolk, A. E. (1993) *Educational psychology*. Boston, MA: Allyn and Bacon.

Woollard, J. (2010) *Psychology for the classroom: behaviourism*. London: Routledge.

Wray, D. and Lewis, M. (1997) *Extending literacy*. London: Routledge Falmer.

Index